The Constitution of the United States

A LOOK AT THE EIGHTEENTH AND TWENTY-FIRST AMENDMENTS

THE PROHIBITION AND SALE OF INTOXICATING LIQUORS

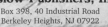

489100240   A look at the Eighteenth and . . .

AMY GRAHAM

MyReportLinks.com Books

an imprint of

Enslow Publishers, Inc.

Box 398, 40 Industrial Road
Berkeley Heights, NJ 07922
USA

Hamilton Southeastern Jr. High

MyReportLinks.com Books, an imprint of Enslow Publishers, Inc. MyReportLinks®
is a registered trademark of Enslow Publishers, Inc.

Library of Congress Cataloging-in-Publication Data

Graham, Amy.
  A look at the Eighteenth and Twenty-first Amendments : the prohibition and sale of intoxicating
liquors / Amy Graham.
      p. cm. — (The Constitution of the United States)
  Includes bibliographical references and index.
  ISBN-13: 978-1-59845-063-7
  ISBN-10: 1-59845-063-8
  1. Prohibition—United States—History—Juvenile literature. I. Title.
HV5089.G63 2007
363.4'1097309042—dc22
                                        2006023965

Printed in the United States of America

10 9 8 7 6 5 4 3 2 1

To Our Readers:
Through the purchase of this book, you and your library gain access to the Report Links that specifically
back up this book.
The Publisher will provide access to the Report Links that back up this book and will keep these Report
Links up to date on **www.myreportlinks.com** for five years from the book's first publication date.
We have done our best to make sure all Internet addresses in this book were active and appropriate when
we went to press. However, the author and the Publisher have no control over, and assume no liability
for, the material available on those Internet sites or on other Web sites they may link to.
The usage of the MyReportLinks.com Books Web site is subject to the terms and conditions stated on the
Usage Policy Statement on **www.myreportlinks.com.**
A password may be required to access the Report Links that back up this book. The password is found
on the bottom of page 4 of this book.
Any comments or suggestions can be sent by e-mail to comments@myreportlinks.com or to the address
on the back cover.

Photo Credits: Al Capone Museum, p. 54; Amanda Hendrick/West Virginia University, p. 14; Brown
University Library, p. 63; Carl H. Miller, p. 61; Courtroom Television Network LLC, p. 45; Doug Lindner,
University of Missouri-Kansas City Law School, p. 79; Herbert Hoover Presidential Library &
Museum/National Archives, p. 86; KCET/PBS Online, p. 33; LexisNexis, p. 82; Library of Congress,
pp. 8, 16, 20, 29, 30–31, 36, 40, 46, 48, 50–51, 58–59, 64–65, 67, 74, 76–77, 80–81, 84–85, 90, 94–95;
MyReportLinks.com Books, p. 4; National Archives, pp. 1, 44, 97, 104; Ohio Historical Society, p. 34;
OSU Department of History, p. 71; Photos.com, p. 102–103; Prof. D. J. Hanson, p. 12; Project Gutenberg
Library Archive Foundation, p. 21; Roosevelt University, p. 93; Schaffer Library of Drug Policy, pp. 11, 49;
Society for the History of Technology (SHOT), p. 26; Stockbyte Sensitive Issues, p. 106–107; Thomas
Hunt, p. 57; Thomson FindLaw, pp. 39, 99; U.S. Department of Justice, p. 55; U.S. Government Printing
Office, p. 72; Westerville Public Library, p. 32; Whiskey Rebellion, p. 25; World Book, Inc., p. 19.

Cover Photo: Library of Congress

CONTENTS

MyReportLinks.com Books
Great Books, Great Links, Great for Research!

The Internet sites featured in this book can save you hours of research time. These Internet sites—we call them **"Report Links"**—are constantly changing, but we keep them up to date on our Web site.

When you see this "Approved Web Site" logo, you will know that we are directing you to a great Internet site that will help you with your research.

Give it a try! Type **http://www.myreportlinks.com** into your browser, click on the series title and enter the password, then click on the book title, and scroll down to the Report Links listed for this book.

The Report Links will bring you to great source documents, photographs, and illustrations. MyReportLinks.com Books save you time, feature Report Links that are kept up to date, and make report writing easier than ever! A complete listing of the Report Links can be found on pages 116–117 at the back of the book.

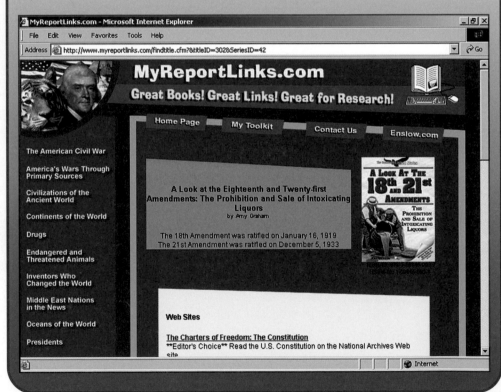

Please see "To Our Readers" on the copyright page for important information about this book, the MyReportLinks.com Web site, and the Report Links that back up this book.

Please enter **ETA1229** if asked for a password.

TIME LINE

1784 —American Dr. Benjamin Rush announces that alcoholism is a disease.

1851 —State of Maine becomes the first state to ban the sale of liquor.

1872 —National Prohibition Party runs a candidate in the presidential election.

1873 —The Women's Crusade closes saloons with street
–1874 demonstrations.

1874 —The Women's Christian Temperance Union is founded.

1880 —Kansas amends its state constitution to prohibit liquor.

1893 —The powerful Anti-Saloon League is founded in Oberlin, Ohio.

1913 —Anti-Saloon League holds Jubilee Convention celebrating twentieth anniversary.

—Webb-Kenyon Act makes it illegal to transport liquor into "dry" states.

1914 —World War I breaks out in Europe.

1917 —United States enters World War I.

—Food Control Act outlaws using grains to make alcohol.

—Congress considers a bill to amend the Constitution to ban alcohol.

1919 —Prohibition becomes Eighteenth Amendment to the Constitution.

—Congress passes the National Prohibition Act (Volstead Act).

1920 —National Census taken: More Americans live in urban than rural areas for the first time ever.

—The Twentieth Amendment to the Constitution passes, giving women the right to vote.

1921 —Congress passes the Willis-Campbell Act (Emergency Beer Act).

1925 —Carroll Decision: The Supreme Court strengthens police powers of search and seizure.

1928 —*Olmstead* v. *the United States:* The Supreme Court upholds police wiretapping of private phone lines.

1929 —Congress passes the Jones Act, increasing jail terms and fines for Prohibition law offenders.

1930 —Prohibition Bureau is transferred from the IRS to the Justice Department. ·

1931 —Wickersham Commission publishes its report on crime.

1932 —Presidential candidate Franklin D. Roosevelt speaks against Prohibition.

1933 —*April:* President Roosevelt declares beer to be legal.

—*June:* Half the Prohibition agents are dismissed.

—*December:* The Twenty-first Amendment is ratified, ending Prohibition.

WOMEN UNITE AGAINST THE DEMON RUM

1

A band of women marched down the center of the street, their voices raised in song. The hems of their long skirts swooshed through the mud. They locked arms with one another to help them feel safe. They were headed into a seedy part of town. There, in the saloons, men spent their hard-earned wages on beer and whiskey. Alone, not one of these women would dare go there. Proper women did not go to saloons. Marching together, they had no fears. They felt like nothing could stop them. They were on a mission to change their town once and for all. These women had just come from a meeting at a church. They had listened raptly to a speech about the evils of alcohol. Now they were ready to do their part in the war against the saloons.

➔ THE PROBLEM WITH ALCOHOL

In America in the mid 1800s, alcohol was a very common drink. Some people were even paid their wages

Starting in the mid 1800s, women formed groups to battle the societal ills caused by too much alcohol consumption. This sketch, showing a woman bashing barrels of booze, is called Woman's Holy War. *It was published in 1874.*

partly in liquor instead of money. Beer, wine, hard cider, rum, whiskey, bourbon—folks drank all kinds of liquor. Some took a nip with every meal, even breakfast. They thought it was good for their health.[1] Doctors agreed. They often gave it to their patients as a medicine. They thought it could cure all sorts of illnesses.

Even so, people also knew that too much alcohol was bad. When people drink too much of it, their brains do not work properly. Their minds become muddled. Their bodies are slow to react. When they are drunk, people do things they would not normally do. They can lose their sense of what is right and what is wrong. Alcohol is also addictive. People who drink a lot of alcohol can start to crave it. Someone who is addicted to alcohol is called an alcoholic. If an alcoholic does not drink it every day, he feels very sick. Yet if he does drink it every day, the alcohol slowly destroys his body. The human body needs to drink water to work well, not alcohol. Most people understood that too much alcohol is bad for people's health.

The man who gave the speech to the women at the church was Dr. Dio Lewis. Lewis traveled all over the United States in the mid-to-late 1800s. Everywhere he went he gave speeches about alcohol and how it must be stopped. Dr. Lewis told the crowd that alcohol was the work of the devil. He urged them not to sit idly by and watch alcohol ruin their men. They had the power to get rid of alcohol, he said, if only they would act. Lewis knew it could work. When he was a boy, his father would often come home drunk. One day his mother had had enough. She got together with other fed-up wives. They convinced the local saloon keeper to close up shop. Lewis shared his mother's story.[2] He told the people at the church they could do it, too. Not only could they, they must. As good Christian women, he convinced them that they had a duty to God to rid their town of alcohol.

→SHUTTING DOWN THE SALOON

As the women drew closer, they could smell the stench of the saloons. On this one street, there were a dozen places to buy a drink. None of them were respectable. A thick layer of sawdust covered the saloon floor. It soaked up the spilled drinks and tobacco juice. One drunken man lay senseless in an alleyway. A dirty urchin boy was searching through the drunkard's pockets. Two men who could barely stand were yelling and throwing punches at each other. They stopped and stared when they heard the women singing. The women came to a halt outside the worst of the saloons. A pyramid of beer bottles stood on the windowsill, blocking the view of the bar. From inside came the sounds of swear words and barroom songs. The women kneeled down on the muddy

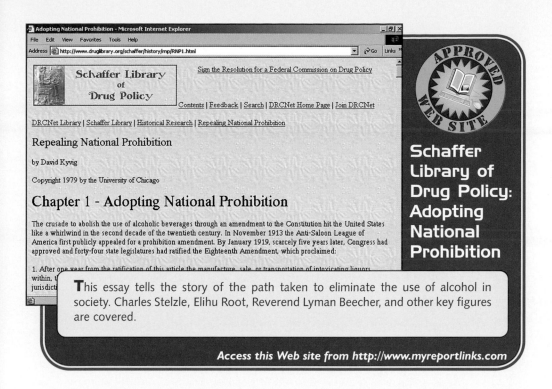

Adopting National Prohibition - Microsoft Internet Explorer

File   Edit   View   Favorites   Tools   Help

Address http://www.druglibrary.org/schaffer/history/mp/RNP1.html

Schaffer Library
of
Drug Policy

Sign the Resolution for a Federal Commission on Drug Policy

Contents | Feedback | Search | DRCNet Home Page | Join DRCNet

DRCNet Library | Schaffer Library | Historical Research | Repealing National Prohibition

Repealing National Prohibition

by David Kyvig

Copyright 1979 by the University of Chicago

Chapter 1 - Adopting National Prohibition

The crusade to abolish the use of alcoholic beverages through an amendment to the Constitution hit the United States like a whirlwind in the second decade of the twentieth century. In November 1913 the Anti-Saloon League of America first publicly appealed for a prohibition amendment. By January 1919, scarcely five years later, Congress had approved and forty-four state legislatures had ratified the Eighteenth Amendment, which proclaimed:

1. After one year from the ratification of this article the manufacture, sale, or transportation of intoxicating liquors within, t...
jurisdict...

Schaffer Library of Drug Policy: Adopting National Prohibition

This essay tells the story of the path taken to eliminate the use of alcohol in society. Charles Stelzle, Elihu Root, Reverend Lyman Beecher, and other key figures are covered.

Access this Web site from http://www.myreportlinks.com

street outside the saloon door. They folded their hands before their faces in prayer. They prayed to God that He would close the saloon forever. They wanted the men inside to return home to their families. They wanted them to never drink again. They did not like their husbands to drink alcohol. When they came home drunk, sometimes they were mean. Sometimes they had no money left to buy food.[3] The women had lost all patience. The saloon was the root of their trouble. If only there was no such thing as liquor! Things had to change.

The saloon keeper swung open the shuttered door. "Go home, women!" he hollered. "This is no place for you! Mind your own business and go back to your homes! I have a right to run a business!" Some of the men inside began to yell, too. The women did not budge. They felt God would protect them. When they started to sing another hymn, some of the men grew quiet. Maybe the women were right. Maybe rum was a demon, tempting them to act badly. Some men hung their heads in shame. They left the saloon and did not look back. Other men thought the women were crazy. This was no way for women to act, telling men what to do! They ignored the women and went right on drinking. Still, it was not quite as enjoyable with the women right outside the door, shouting out Psalms from the Bible.

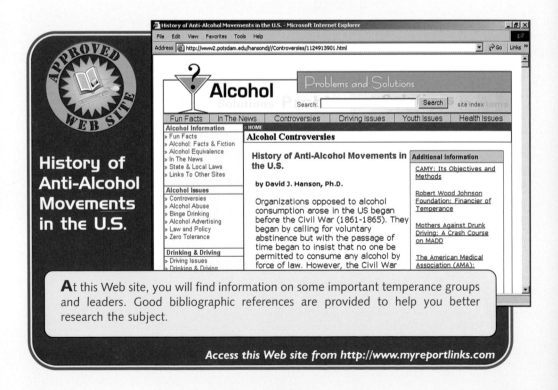

History of Anti-Alcohol Movements in the U.S.

At this Web site, you will find information on some important temperance groups and leaders. Good bibliographic references are provided to help you better research the subject.

Access this Web site from http://www.myreportlinks.com

➔ TAKING THE PLEDGE

The women would not be stopped. At church the following Sunday, they struck again. They told everyone which men had been to the saloons. These men felt guilty and ashamed. Their minister and the congregation all urged them to give up drinking. So, many men took a pledge not to drink anymore. They signed their names on a piece of paper. If they agreed to totally give up all alcohol, they had a "T" written by their name. These people became known as teetotalers.

All during the week, small groups of women stood outside the saloons. They asked the men headed in to drink to reconsider. If they loved Jesus, the women argued, they should sign the pledge not to drink. Some men just kept walking through the door into the saloon. Others snuck in through a back door to avoid the women. Some of the women even went right into the saloons and sat down. They tried to shame any man who dared come in to buy a drink. To the dismay of the saloon keepers, fewer and fewer men came out to the saloons. Some men were moved by the women's appeal. Others stopped going because they did not want to argue with the women. It was not worth the fight. Many saloons closed their doors for good. Sometimes the saloon keepers found different jobs. Other times they merely moved to a different town, or quietly reopened

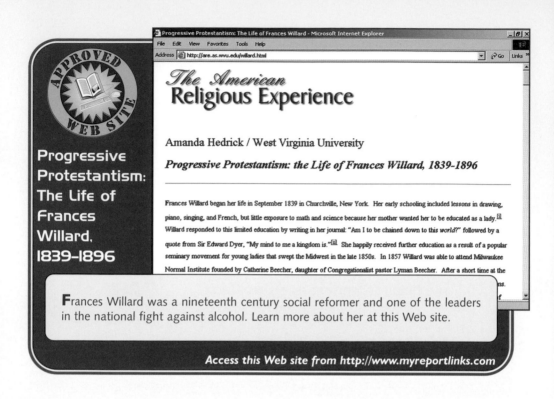

Progressive
Protestantism:
The Life of
Frances
Willard,
1839-1896

The American
Religious Experience

Amanda Hedrick / West Virginia University

Progressive Protestantism: the Life of Frances Willard, 1839-1896

Frances Willard began her life in September 1839 in Churchville, New York. Her early schooling included lessons in drawing, piano, singing, and French, but little exposure to math and science because her mother wanted her to be educated as a lady. [1] Willard responded to this limited education by writing in her journal: "Am I to be chained down to this *world*?" followed by a quote from Sir Edward Dyer, "My mind to me a kingdom is."[2] She happily received further education as a result of a popular seminary movement for young ladies that swept the Midwest in the late 1850s. In 1857 Willard was able to attend Milwaukee Normal Institute founded by Catherine Beecher, daughter of Congregationalist pastor Lyman Beecher. After a short time at the

Frances Willard was a nineteenth century social reformer and one of the leaders in the national fight against alcohol. Learn more about her at this Web site.

Access this Web site from http://www.myreportlinks.com

under a new name. One thing was for sure: The women had people talking.

This group of righteous women was part of a movement that swept across the nation in the late 1800s. Women in many towns got together to protest the saloons. They called themselves the Women's Crusade. They were very dedicated. They kept up their protest, even when people yelled at them. Sometimes angry mobs threw things at them or tried to hurt them. The movement was most strong in the Midwestern states. Women there succeeded in closing thousands of saloons, at least for a while.

➡ TEMPERANCE MOVEMENT

The Women's Crusade was a new solution to an old concern. Americans had worried about alcohol abuse for quite some time. Church sermons often called for temperance. Temperance means that people should not drink too much, if at all. Many churches encouraged their members to take a pledge not to drink. People also joined groups to stop alcohol abuse. The Washingtonians were one such club.

The Washingtonians were a men's group. The members vowed not to drink alcohol. They believed alcohol led to poverty and crime. Oddly they chose to name themselves after the first president. It is unclear why they chose Washington as their hero. Washington did drink alcohol. He even owned a distillery to make his own alcohol. The Washingtonians and other groups were part of a temperance movement. Americans wanted to shape their young country into a good place to live. They looked to their churches to teach them right from wrong. Then they tried to shape their society according to those principles. For instance, many Americans believed slavery was evil. They spoke out to abolish slavery. They worked together in groups to end slavery. Now these same moral Americans had a new cause to fight for. They would work together to bring an end to the Demon Rum.

As a rule, the temperance movement did not try to ban all alcohol. They wanted to teach people about the evils of alcohol. They hoped people would make the right decision about whether or not to drink alcohol. The Women's Crusade took it further. They wanted to prohibit, or ban, all kinds of alcoholic drinks. They were not temperance workers. They were a new kind of alcohol opponent: the prohibitionists.

WHITE RIBBONERS

Women saw that they could be powerful when they worked together. Traditionally, women

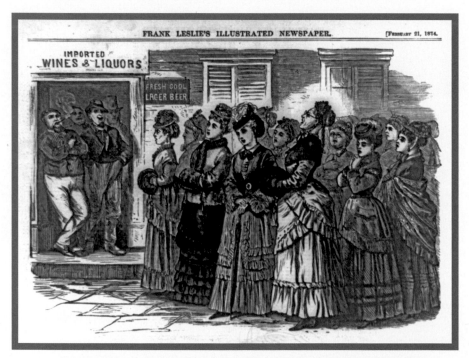

▲ Artist S. B. Morton created this image depicting the women of Logan, Ohio, as they sang hymns in front of the town's barrooms. They were hoping to make the people inside feel guilty about being there.

stayed at home. They did not have public lives. They could not vote. They could be active in their churches, but they never held public office. Street protests and marches were the only way they could be heard. Some people said it was unseemly for women to march in public. These women felt strongly about closing saloons. They knew their message was important. They wanted more of a say in the way their society ran.

To this end, they formed the Woman's Christian Temperance Union (WCTU) in 1874. It soon had chapters all across America. Their symbol was a white ribbon. In the words of their president, they believed that women were "truest to God and our country."[4] They thought American society needed to listen to the voices of women. Banning alcohol was one of their goals. They also worked for many other causes. They helped to improve working conditions in factories. They campaigned to make it illegal for children to work.

It was common for poor families to send their children to work in the factories. The children often worked in poor conditions. They had to work long hours. They did not earn as much pay as the adults who did the same job.

The WCTU helped people to see that child labor is wrong. The WCTU also thought women should have the right to vote. They made enemies along the way. The brewers and distillers who made beer and alcohol did not want women to get the vote.[5] They were sure if women got the vote, alcohol would soon be outlawed.

SWINGING THE HATCHET

Carry Amelia Nation was one of the most infamous women to fight for the cause. In her home state of Kansas, saloons were against the law. This did not stop people from drinking in public. The police did not enforce the law. Saloons were still running out in the open in many towns. Nation's first husband, Dr. Charles Gloyd, had been an alcoholic. He drank himself to death. The couple had a young daughter who suffered from poor health. Nation thought her husband's drinking and smoking were to blame. Though Nation soon remarried a minister, she never lost her anger about alcohol. Nation felt strongly that alcohol should be illegal. She led a chapter of the local Woman's Christian Temperance Union. One day Nation believed she heard God speaking to her. He commanded her to go to the town of Kiowa, Kansas, and close the saloons.

Carry Nation hopped in her horse-drawn buggy and sped off to Kiowa. She did not tell anyone what she was about to do. She stormed into a Kiowa saloon all by herself. She was a woman in her fifties. She wore spectacles, and her gray hair was drawn up severely in a bun. Still, when she told the bartender to stand back, he did. She had a fire in her eyes that declared her dangerous. Nation smashed the mirror behind the bar with a rock. Then she set to work on the bottles of liquor. Soon the saloon floor was afloat in a large puddle of alcohol and broken glass. She destroyed three saloons that day before the police came to stop her. She had broken the law by destroying another person's property. Needless to say, the police let her go. If they had been doing their jobs, there would have been no saloons in the first place since they were illegal in Kansas.

Kiowa was just the beginning for Carry Nation. She went from city to city attacking the saloons.

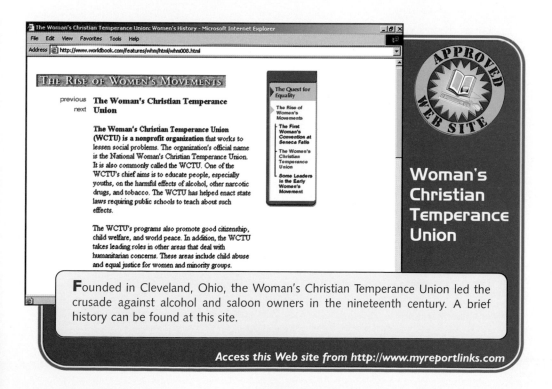

Woman's Christian Temperance Union

Founded in Cleveland, Ohio, the Woman's Christian Temperance Union led the crusade against alcohol and saloon owners in the nineteenth century. A brief history can be found at this site.

Access this Web site from http://www.myreportlinks.com

Her hatchet became her symbol. She also used iron bars, bats, rocks, and bottles. She hacked the bar stools and pool tables into splinters. Her fervor was so terrifying that most people stayed out of her path. Sometimes the police came to restore order. Nation was not sorry for the destruction she caused. She felt that it was perfectly all right to use force to shut down saloons. After all, if the police had only done their job, she would not need

▲ Carry Nation was famous for storming into saloons with an axe in an attempt to destroy them. Her first husband had been an alcoholic and she had been upset about it ever since. She is shown here with an unidentified man.

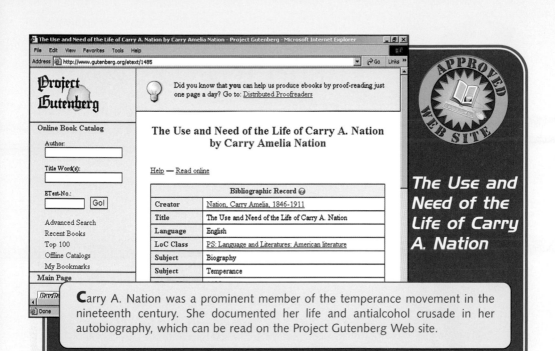

The Use and Need of the Life of Carry A. Nation by Carry Amelia Nation - Project Gutenberg - Microsoft Internet Explorer

File   Edit   View   Favorites   Tools   Help

Address http://www.gutenberg.org/etext/1485   Go   Links »

Project Gutenberg

Did you know that **you** can help us produce ebooks by proof-reading just one page a day? Go to: Distributed Proofreaders

Online Book Catalog

Author:

Title Word(s):

EText-No.:   Go!

Advanced Search
Recent Books
Top 100
Offline Catalogs
My Bookmarks

Main Page

The Use and Need of the Life of Carry A. Nation by Carry Amelia Nation

Help — Read online

Bibliographic Record ⊘	
Creator	Nation, Carry Amelia, 1846-1911
Title	The Use and Need of the Life of Carry A. Nation
Language	English
LoC Class	PS: Language and Literatures: American literature
Subject	Biography
Subject	Temperance

The Use and Need of the Life of Carry A. Nation

Carry A. Nation was a prominent member of the temperance movement in the nineteenth century. She documented her life and antialcohol crusade in her autobiography, which can be read on the Project Gutenberg Web site.

Access this Web site from http://www.myreportlinks.com

her hatchet. Nation would tell the police they could not charge her for closing a saloon they should have closed themselves. She was thrown in jail several times. She would fall to her knees on the jail floor and pray. Perhaps her prayers paid off, for she was never charged with a crime.

Carry A. Nation was a folk hero to some. Other people thought she did more harm than good. Even people who wanted to outlaw alcohol did not always agree with her violent ways. They did not want the public to think that all women crusaders were lawbreakers. Most of the prohibitionists felt solemn prayer and public protest were better ways to close saloons.

2 TEMPERANCE AND TEETOTALERS

The liquor trade is a big business. Like any legal business, it pays taxes to the government. When people make or sell alcohol, they must pay a tax. Tax dollars go to fund the government. As early as the 1790s, the United States charged a whiskey tax. Whiskey is a strong alcoholic drink. It is made by distilling a grain, such as corn, rye, or barley. The new tax made farmers of Pennsylvania angry. Had they not just fought a war over paying taxes to the King of England? America was now a free country. Yet the new United States was acting like the king, they said. There was a nine-cent tax on every gallon of alcohol. The farmers did not think the tax was fair. The new government could not tell them what to do. They could not force them to pay the tax!

An angry mob came out to protest. There were seven thousand people in all. President George Washington had to send out troops. A huge army marched out to quell the uprising which came to be

22

known as the Whisky Rebellion. The soldiers were able to convince the farmers to go home. After that, the farmers paid their taxes. By 1914, more than a third of the government's income came from the liquor business.[1]

➔Beyond Moral Suasion

Temperance groups wanted to teach people why alcohol was bad. They hoped to persuade folks not to drink. They called this tactic "moral suasion." But moral suasion only took the cause so far. Liquor was still a problem. A growing number of teetotalers felt they needed a stronger tool.[2] If they could not convince people to give up liquor, they would force them to. They turned to the law. If enough people in a town did not want alcohol, they could ban it. People passed laws in their towns to outlaw saloons. This new tactic was referred to as the "local option." Citizens could decide for themselves, on a local level. It seemed to work. Towns had laws that the local people could agree on. Around the country, people began to talk. Maybe laws could solve the problem. Maybe laws could rid communities of alcohol once and for all.

It was not long before people tried to make statewide laws to ban alcohol. Maine was the first to do so. The "Maine law" passed in 1851. All across the state, it was against the law to sell alcohol. There were a few exceptions to the rule. It was still legal to sell alcohol if it was used as medicine. In 1880, the state of Kansas even went a step further. They did not just pass a law. They wrote the ban into their state's constitution. A constitution is a powerful set of laws. It lays out the way the government works. It was against the supreme law of the state to make or sell liquor. Two years later, the people of Iowa did the same. They voted to amend, or change, their constitution to ban alcohol. In the 1880s, laws prohibiting the sale of spirits cropped up all over the United States.

→ THE INDUSTRIAL REVOLUTION

As the eighteenth century drew to an end, things were changing in America. Americans were doing new kinds of work. Many people left their farms in the country. They moved to towns and cities where they could find work in factories. Immigrants came to America from other countries. They found work at the mills, too. People had to work with big, heavy machines at the mills. The workers had to pay close attention to their work. When they did not, there were accidents. Workers got hurt. People who were drunk at work could not do their job safely. It was much too dangerous.

Between 1911 and 1920, Congress tried to change factory conditions. They wrote worker's compensation laws. The new laws helped to protect the rights of workers. Companies would now

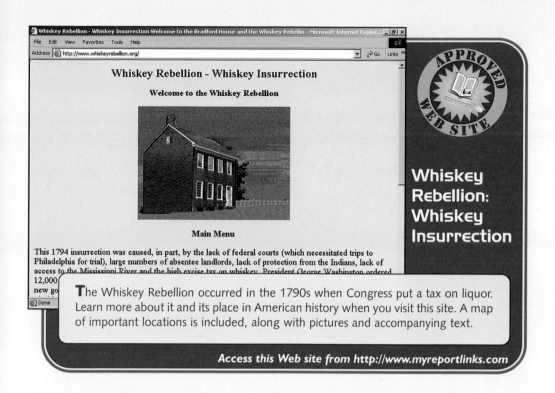

Whiskey Rebellion - Whiskey Insurrection - Welcome to the Bradford House and the Whiskey Rebellio - Microsoft Internet Explor...

File   Edit   View   Favorites   Tools   Help

Address http://www.whiskeyrebellion.org/

Whiskey Rebellion - Whiskey Insurrection

Welcome to the Whiskey Rebellion

Main Menu

This 1794 insurrection was caused, in part, by the lack of federal courts (which necessitated trips to Philadelphia for trial), large numbers of absentee landlords, lack of protection from the Indians, lack of access to the Mississippi River and the high excise tax on whiskey. President George Washington ordered 12,000 new go

Done

Whiskey Rebellion: Whiskey Insurrection

The Whiskey Rebellion occurred in the 1790s when Congress put a tax on liquor. Learn more about it and its place in American history when you visit this site. A map of important locations is included, along with pictures and accompanying text.

Access this Web site from http://www.myreportlinks.com

have to pay a worker who was hurt on the job. They had to pay him even if he was too hurt to work ever again. They could not fire him. The factories had to take a new approach to safety. They made very strict rules. They were meant to prevent accidents. They helped to teach people about the dangers of drinking liquor.[3]

→ THE LECTURE CIRCUIT

Have you ever wondered what it was like in the days before television and radio? What did people do for fun? One thing they did was attend lectures. Speakers traveled from town to town. They gave lectures about many topics. Temperance was

Unit 2: Early Industrialization - Microsoft Internet Explorer

File   Edit   View   Favorites   Tools   Help

Address http://invention.smithsonian.org/centerpieces/whole_cloth/u2ei/index.html   Go   Links

[Home]   [Units]   [Timeline]   [Forums]   [Resources]   [Index]

EARLY   Unit Two

Unit "at a Glance"

Essays

Activities

▶Mechanization

▶Factories/Environment

▶Labor and Industrial Life

Glossary

Bibliography

Unit Two

EARLY INDUSTRIALIZATION

Wool Carding Machine

Abraham Rees, Woolen Manufacture, "Carding Engine," Cyclopedia, volume 4, 1822.
Courtesy of the American Textile History Museum, Lowell, Mass.

[Teacher Essay]   [Student Essays]

Done

The Smithsonian Institution has put together the **Early Industrialization** Web site on the Industrial Revolution and how it began. Essays and teachers' notes accompany the material, as do archival images.

a popular subject. Dr. Dio Lewis, who encouraged the women to close saloons, was one such speaker. John Bartholomew Gough was another man who drew big crowds. Gough started his career as a stage actor in comedies. He did not make much money acting, though. He got addicted to drink and could not hold down a job. Later he turned his life around. He gave up alcohol and toured the nation as a temperance speaker. To be a success, a speaker needed to be entertaining. Gough was certainly that. He told audiences about how low he had sunk as an alcoholic. He told them about how painful it was when he stopped drinking liquor. He told them that it was not safe to drink just a little, now and again. Gough gave it his all. When he stepped off the stage, he was sweaty and exhausted. People loved him. He grew quite wealthy.

There was no lack of people speaking about the sins of Demon Rum. There was money to be made. While the talks were popular, not many drunks heard them.[4] Alcoholics went to saloons, not church meetings. Instead, it was the average person who heard these speakers. They were moved by what they heard. They wanted to do their part to close the saloons. If only no one sold liquor, then no one would get addicted to it. Or so they reasoned.

NATIONAL PROHIBITION PARTY

Men began to vote for candidates based on whether they were "wet" or "dry." "Dry" meant that the person believed Prohibition was a good idea. "Wet" meant that they did not support banning alcohol. It was a heated topic of debate. Neither the Republicans nor the Democrats would take a stand. They feared that they might alienate the wets or the drys. The drys grew frustrated. They formed their own group, the Prohibition Party, in Ohio. It soon spread to other states in the Midwest. The party even ran a teetotaler for president of the

United States in 1872. The party never did very well. It did prove one thing: Some people felt very strongly about Prohibition. They would vote on that one issue over all others. From their view, alcohol was the biggest problem of their time.

OBERLIN AND THE ANTI-SALOON LEAGUE OF OHIO

Oberlin College in Ohio has often led the nation. It was the first to admit women. People there took a strong stance against slavery. Oberlin took the stage yet again in 1893. A group of men began to meet. They talked about the evils of rum and what they could do to stop it. The group took the name the Anti-Saloon League. It quickly grew. Within two years, it had members all over the nation. It was a lot like the Woman's Christian Temperance League. The two groups often worked together. But the men's league was unlike the WCTU, as well. The WCTU worked on many social issues. The Anti-Saloon League had just one goal. They wanted to see the end of the American saloon.

Wayne B. Wheeler was the general counsel for the Anti-Saloon League. He had studied at Oberlin College and had become caught up in the cause. He knew firsthand of the evils of alcohol. When he was a child, a farmhand drove a pitchfork through Wheeler's leg. It was an accident. The man had been drunk. Wheeler never forgot the incident. He

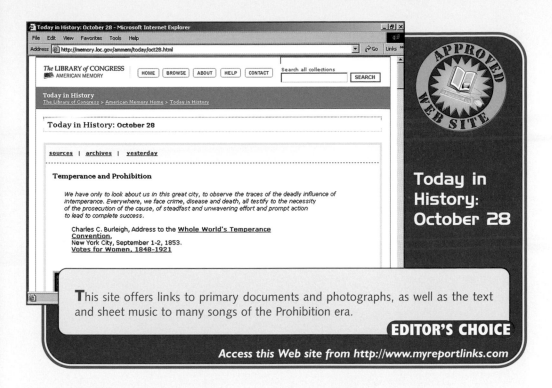

Today in History: October 28 - Microsoft Internet Explorer

File   Edit   View   Favorites   Tools   Help

Address http://memory.loc.gov/ammem/today/oct28.html   Go   Links »

The LIBRARY of CONGRESS
AMERICAN MEMORY

HOME   BROWSE   ABOUT   HELP   CONTACT

Search all collections

SEARCH

Today in History
The Library of Congress > American Memory Home > Today in History

Today in History: October 28

sources | archives | yesterday

Temperance and Prohibition

We have only to look about us in this great city, to observe the traces of the deadly influence of intemperance. Everywhere, we face crime, disease and death, all testify to the necessity of the prosecution of the cause, of steadfast and unwavering effort and prompt action to lead to complete success.

Charles C. Burleigh, Address to the **Whole World's Temperance Convention**, New York City, September 1-2, 1853.
Votes for Women, 1848-1921

Today in History: October 28

This site offers links to primary documents and photographs, as well as the text and sheet music to many songs of the Prohibition era.

EDITOR'S CHOICE

Access this Web site from http://www.myreportlinks.com

dedicated his life to banning the Demon Rum. He got a degree in law so he could best serve the league. Wheeler was a force to be reckoned with. According to historian John Kobler, one of his classmates described him as "the locomotive in trousers."[5] He was clever and had a keen sense of politics. He became a very powerful man in Washington, D.C. After all, the Anti-Saloon League had widespread support. They had millions of dollars to spend to further the cause. They even had their own printing press in Westerville, Ohio. It churned out millions of pamphlets, brochures, and books each year. They all had the same message: Alcohol must be stopped.

JUBILEE CONVENTION OF 1913

The Anti-Saloon League held a big event in Columbus, Ohio. They had twenty years of work to be proud of. Thanks to their efforts, many states

had laws on the books banning alcohol. Even in wet states, there were local laws limiting the sale of spirits. At that Jubilee Convention, the league made an important decision. Up until that point, they had worked on the state level. Now the league decided to try a new approach. They set an ambitious goal. They would try to amend the United States Constitution. Why did they not just work to pass a federal law to ban alcohol? A law could easily be changed or even tossed out. An amendment was different. Once it passed, it would be nearly impossible to change. That was the way to go. Members of the league returned home to set to work. With a strong effort, Prohibition would soon be the law of the land. The future would bring a new era of reform.

➡ WEBB-KENYON LAW

It was against the law to sell or make alcohol in many states. That did not mean people who lived there could not drink alcohol. There was no law saying

In the 1870s, politicians began taking sides for or against Prohibition. One of the "Drys" was South Dakota governor Peter Norbeck. In this photograph, he is shown signing his state's "bone dry" law in 1917.

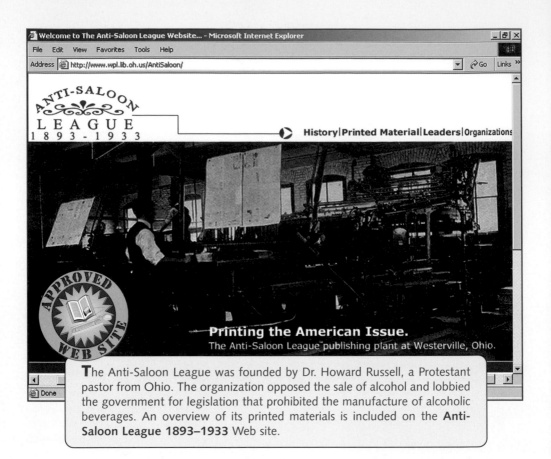

Welcome to The Anti-Saloon League Website... - Microsoft Internet Explorer

File   Edit   View   Favorites   Tools   Help

Address http://www.wpl.lib.oh.us/AntiSaloon/

ANTI-SALOON
LEAGUE
1 8 9 3 - 1 9 3 3

History | Printed Material | Leaders | Organizations

APPROVED WEB SITE

Printing the American Issue.
The Anti-Saloon League publishing plant at Westerville, Ohio.

The Anti-Saloon League was founded by Dr. Howard Russell, a Protestant pastor from Ohio. The organization opposed the sale of alcohol and lobbied the government for legislation that prohibited the manufacture of alcoholic beverages. An overview of its printed materials is included on the **Anti-Saloon League 1893–1933** Web site.

one could not buy or drink alcohol. People simply went to a state where they could buy it. They stocked up. Drys saw this as flouting the law. If a state was dry, then whose job was it to keep alcohol from coming across the border? The drys appealed to Congress. The Webb-Kenyon Act passed in 1913. It made it illegal to carry alcohol into a dry state. President Woodrow Wilson vetoed the bill. He thought it was unconstitutional. Congress did not agree. They passed the act over his veto.

→ World War I

When World War I broke out in Europe in 1914, Americans were called on to help. Because of the war, European farmers could not grow crops. There was not enough food to feed everyone. Americans vowed to conserve. They would use only what they had to. Then they would send the extra food to their European allies. The Anti-Saloon League saw its chance. If there was ever a time to push an amendment through, it was now. Americans were swept up in the spirit of conserving

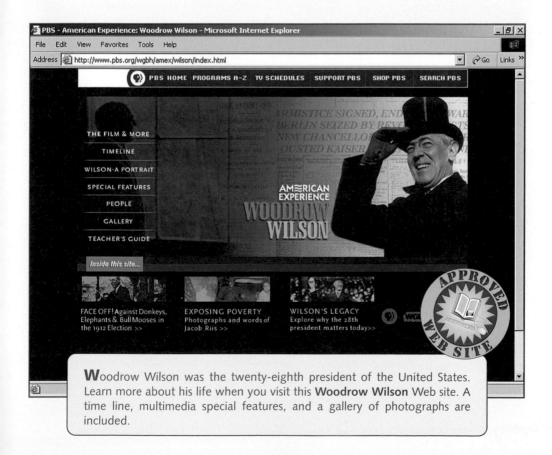

Woodrow Wilson was the twenty-eighth president of the United States. Learn more about his life when you visit this **Woodrow Wilson** Web site. A time line, multimedia special features, and a gallery of photographs are included.

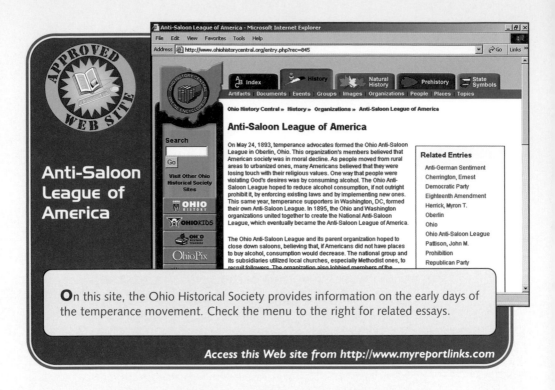

Anti-Saloon League of America

On this site, the Ohio Historical Society provides information on the early days of the temperature movement. Check the menu to the right for related essays.

Access this Web site from http://www.myreportlinks.com

for the war effort. All the grain that was used to make alcohol would be better used to feed people, they argued. The Food Control Act passed in August 1917. The act said it was against the law to use grains to make alcohol. People did not give it much notice. They were too distracted by the war.

→ SPEAKING UP AGAINST PROHIBITION

Of course, saloon keepers did not want to close for good. The beer brewers did not want to shut down. Neither did the whiskey distillers. What would the grape farmers and wine makers do? All these people would lose their jobs. They would lose the livelihoods they had trained for. What would they do for work if liquor was banned? They joined together. They formed groups such as the United States Brewers Association and the Distillers Association of America. They lobbied Congress. They said it was their right to make alcohol. The federal government could not tell the states that alcohol was illegal. Or could it?

The brewers and the distillers had some good points. They spent a lot of money in Washington. They tried to get people to see their point of view. However, they did not get a whole lot of sympathy. The drys had a lot to say in response. For instance, the saloons were a disgrace. Why had they not tried to clean them up? After all, the breweries owned many of the saloons. Now they were complaining that they would lose their profits? Did they think anyone was going to feel sorry for them? Alcohol abuse cost tax payers millions of dollars every year. To complain about a lack of profits did seem a bit crass.

➔POPULAR OPINION

Then there was the link between the liquor trade and the Germans. This also worked against those fighting Prohibition. Beer has been a proud part of Germany's culture for a long time. Many Germans came to America to work in the mills. They brought their beer traditions with them. They did not want to forget their history. So they started a

VOL. XXXVII. No. 959.   PUCK BUILDING, New York, July 24th, 1895.   PRICE 10 CENTS.
Copyright, 1895, by Keppler & Schwarzmann.

"What Fools these Mortals be."

Puck

Entered at N. Y. P. O. as Second-class Mail Matter.

This illustration appeared in Puck magazine on July 24, 1895. It shows a liquor store owner closing his establishment while a "wet" politician suggests that things could change if he were voted back into office.

A RATIONAL LAW, OR —— TAMMANY.

TAMMANY. — Goin' to wait till dem reformers repeal dat law, are yer? Put me back and you won't need no repeal! See?

group to celebrate their culture. It was called the German American Alliance. Many brewers were a part of this group. Other people did not understand. Americans and Germans were enemies. The two countries were at war. Many people saw the German brewers as the enemy, too.[6]

What about the typical American on the street? How did he feel about Prohibition? Certainly not all Americans thought it was a good idea to ban all liquor. In fact, it was a very unpopular idea in big cities like Chicago and New York. Some people did not believe there was anything wrong with an occasional drink. Just because a person had a drink, that should not make him or her a criminal. A total ban on alcohol did not seem possible. It went too far. Wets thought the law would never pass. Still, very few people spoke out against the idea. Perhaps they were afraid of being seen as supporters of the saloons. Maybe they did not really believe the law would ever pass. They thought it was just part of the uproar about the war. If they thought that, they were dead wrong. Little did they know just how quickly things were about to change.

3 THE DEATH OF JOHN BARLEYCORN

The Anti-Saloon League was determined. They would make Prohibition the law of the land. They set to work making it happen. Just a few weeks after the Jubilee Convention, they had put the wheels in motion. They held a grand parade at the nation's Capitol. Women from the WCTU joined them. A total of over four thousand people marched. They sang songs and waved banners. Senator Morris Sheppard brought a bill to the floor of the Senate later that day. The bill proposed a change to the Constitution. The amendment would ban the sale of liquor. The Texas senator did not write the bill himself. The Anti-Saloon League wrote it. They gave it to him at the parade.[1] They gave the same bill to Congressman Richmond Hobson of Alabama. He did his part by introducing the bill to the members of the House of Representatives. When the House voted on the bill, it did not pass. In order to pass, the bill would have needed two thirds of the votes. It did not get enough. Still, it got the support of more than half of the representatives. The league saw it would need to elect more people who would vote dry. It spent a lot of money to support the right candidates. Wayne Wheeler later said their expenses reached an all-time high during this period. The league spent about $2.5 million a year.[2] In the election of 1916, the league got its wish. The drys won the most seats in Congress. The time was ripe for a constitutional ban on liquor.

→THE PROPOSED AMENDMENT

The final amendment was short. It had three simple paragraphs. The first section said that it would be against the law to make, sell, or carry liquor anywhere in the United States. It did not say that

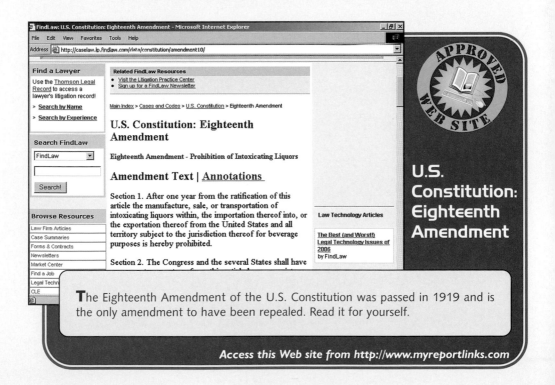

The Eighteenth Amendment of the U.S. Constitution was passed in 1919 and is the only amendment to have been repealed. Read it for yourself.

Access this Web site from http://www.myreportlinks.com

This famous photograph shows a tombstone that was erected in Meriden, Connecticut. John Barleycorn was a fictional character that represented alcohol. The people who erected this tombstone were not happy about Prohibition.

IN MEMORIAM

JOHN BARLEYCORN

BORN B. C.

DIED JAN. 16, 1920

RESURRECTION ?

Silver City Men Erect Barleycorn Monument.

The monument dedicated to John Barleycorn was unveiled with appropriate ceremonies recently, on the grounds of the 1711 Club in Meriden, Conn. Many chief mourners were in attendance.

(Photo from Keystone View Company)

all liquor was illegal. Only liquor that was used "for beverage purposes" would be against the law. It also did not make it against the law to drink or buy liquor. After all, if the amendment passed, there would soon be no liquor to drink. The law would not take effect right away. It allowed for one year. That would give the liquor trade some time to close down.

⊜ ENFORCEMENT

The second part was just one sentence long. It talked about who would have the job of making sure people obeyed the new law. Opponents of the amendment had a good point. They argued that it would give the federal government too much control over the states. Congress saw that this could be a problem. They tried to address this concern here. They made it clear that the states and federal government would have "concurrent power." This phrase was enough to reassure the opponents. Yet, in future years, this part proved tricky. Who was to say what exactly "concurrent power" really meant?

The third section set a time limit. It said that the states had seven years to ratify the amendment. The founding fathers foresaw that the Constitution would need to be changed. They wrote rules about how to amend the Constitution. First an amendment must pass through Congress.

Then it is sent to the states. Each state takes a vote. To pass, the amendment must be accepted by three quarters of the states. If and when that happens, the amendment becomes part of the Constitution. It was the wets who insisted on a time limit. They believed they could block the passage of the amendment. They only needed thirteen states on their side. At the time, there were forty-eight states altogether. The wets were fairly sure they could hold off for seven years. The war years were now drawing to an end. Perhaps some of the excitement would now die down.

⟶ RATIFICATION

The wets had made a serious blunder. There was one major factor that they did not consider. The wets knew just how powerful the Anti-Saloon League was in Washington. Somehow they did not stop to think where the league had begun. For years, it had worked at the state level. The league had strong ties in all of the state capitals. Now it shifted its focus back to the states. Its dream was so close! There was no way the Anti-Saloon League was going to let it slip away. Its hard work paid off. Within thirteen months, three quarters of the states had voted to pass the amendment. The Eighteenth Amendment was added to the Constitution in January 1919. In one year's time, nationwide Prohibition would be the law. In time, all but two of the states voted for the amendment. Rhode Island was the only state to vote against it. Connecticut refused to vote on it at all. America was soon to be a bone-dry nation. The country was stunned at the turn of events. Even its strongest supporters had never dreamed it would pass so soon. Drys were jubilant. Alcohol, and all the problems that went with it, would soon be gone for good.

It was a very simple solution. The drys were confident it would work. Most people who did not agree with the amendment still resigned themselves to it.

➔ THE VOLSTEAD ACT

Now that Prohibition had passed, how would it work? What would be the price for people who broke the law? How serious a crime was it to be? It was up to Congress to say. The job of proposing the new laws fell to a representative from rural Minnesota. His name was Andrew Volstead. He was the head of the Judiciary Committee. Volstead was not a teetotaler. He was known to indulge in a drink every now and then. Yet, for the rest of his life, people linked his name with Prohibition. The new law's official title was the National Prohibition Act. People nicknamed it the Volstead Act. Volstead was not the true author of the act. It was

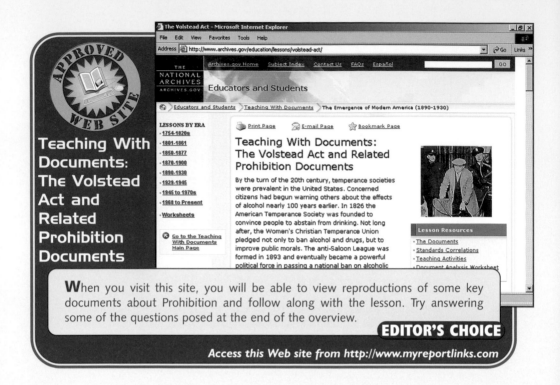

The Volstead Act - Microsoft Internet Explorer

File Edit View Favorites Tools Help

Address http://www.archives.gov/education/lessons/volstead-act/

THE NATIONAL ARCHIVES ARCHIVES.GOV

Archives.gov Home   Subject Index   Contact Us   FAQs   Español   GO

Educators and Students

Educators and Students › Teaching With Documents › The Emergence of Modern America (1890-1930)

Teaching With Documents: The Volstead Act and Related Prohibition Documents

LESSONS BY ERA
- 1754-1820s
- 1801-1861
- 1850-1877
- 1870-1900
- 1890-1930
- 1929-1945
- 1945 to 1970s
- 1968 to Present
- Worksheets

Go to the Teaching With Documents Main Page

Print Page   E-mail Page   Bookmark Page

Teaching With Documents: The Volstead Act and Related Prohibition Documents

By the turn of the 20th century, temperance societies were prevalent in the United States. Concerned citizens had begun warning others about the effects of alcohol nearly 100 years earlier. In 1826 the American Temperance Society was founded to convince people to abstain from drinking. Not long after, the Women's Christian Temperance Union pledged not only to ban alcohol and drugs, but to improve public morals. The anti-Saloon League was formed in 1893 and eventually became a powerful political force in passing a national ban on alcoholic

Lesson Resources
- The Documents
- Standards Correlations
- Teaching Activities
- Document Analysis Worksheet

When you visit this site, you will be able to view reproductions of some key documents about Prohibition and follow along with the lesson. Try answering some of the questions posed at the end of the overview.

EDITOR'S CHOICE

Access this Web site from http://www.myreportlinks.com

Wayne Wheeler of the Anti-Saloon League who wrote it and gave it to Volstead.[3]

The Eighteenth Amendment outlawed the sale of "intoxicating beverages." What kind of drinks did that mean? People were not sure. Some people assumed that it only meant hard liquor, not beer or wine. The Volstead Act quickly set them straight. It meant any drink that had more than one half of one percent of alcohol. In other words, beer and wine would not be allowed, either. The law did make a few exceptions to the rule. A doctor could still prescribe liquor for medicine. A priest could use wine as a sacrament. Of course, industries would still need to use alcohol. Saloons, however, would be shut down once and for all. There were penalties for anyone who was caught breaking the law. Criminals would face fines. They could even go to prison.

→A Demon's Funeral

The law would go into effect at midnight on January 16, 1920. As the date drew closer, wets and drys started to prepare, each in their own ways. Some people wanted to continue to drink liquor in the privacy of their homes. Soon they would no longer be able to buy it. So they bought as much as they could while it was still legal. Vendors sold off their liquor stocks. The drys were busy, too. They were celebrating their win. The folks at one

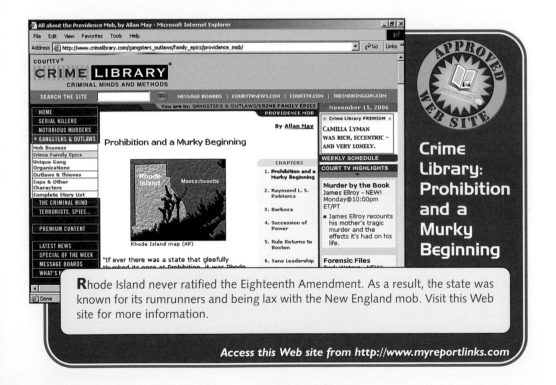

Crime Library: Prohibition and a Murky Beginning

Rhode Island never ratified the Eighteenth Amendment. As a result, the state was known for its rumrunners and being lax with the New England mob. Visit this Web site for more information.

Access this Web site from http://www.myreportlinks.com

church in Norfolk, Virginia, had a lot of fun with it. They held a funeral for the Demon Rum, only they called him "John Barleycorn." It was their way of saying good-bye to the days of legal liquor. They carried a pretend casket through the streets. Someone even dressed up as the devil. He wore horns on his head and danced along behind the casket. The devil pretended to weep and mourn. He was sad about the loss of his good friend, the Demon Rum. When they reached the church, Reverend Billy Sunday gave a fiery sermon. Sunday was a former baseball star who had found religion. "Goodbye, John! You were God's worst enemy. You were Hell's best friend," he roared.[4]

The Dry Years

The Library of Congress Prints and Photographs Division has many photographs and drawings on the subject of the Prohibition. View the selected images and use the search function to find more.

EDITOR'S CHOICE

Access this Web site from http://www.myreportlinks.com

➔A Nation of Criminals

With the new law on the books, the saloons were forced to close. Prohibition agents were out on the streets to make sure people obeyed. They arrested a few people for selling liquor. In general, people respected the new law at first. Yet alcohol did not disappear. However, it no longer came from legal sources. Now it came from criminal sources. It was not just the typical bad guys who were buying liquor on the black market. Ordinary people were breaking the law left and right. When it came right down to it, many people did not think it was wrong to drink alcohol. They did not feel the government should tell them what they could drink. It was too personal a matter.

America had a big problem on its hands. Normally law-abiding citizens were not respecting the law. After all, people obeyed other laws because they agreed with them. They agreed it was bad to steal, so they did not steal. They did not agree that it was wrong to drink, however, so they did not follow the law. Some people thought the law was a good idea—for other people, but not for themselves.

The price of alcohol shot sky-high. Poor people could not afford the high prices. But if a person had the money, it was easy to find someone who would sell him or her some liquor.

▲ *These Prohibition officers are raiding an establishment in Washington, D.C.*

⊖ENFORCING THE LAW

Who was in charge of policing the new law? A new force of three thousand federal agents was. They were the Prohibition Unit. The unit was part of the Internal Revenue Service (IRS). It was strange for that department to have law enforcement officers. Would it not be a better job for the Justice Department? The IRS was overworked as it was. The Volstead Act put it under the IRS, and that is where it stayed for many years. The job of Prohibition agent did not pay very well. The men made anywhere from thirty-five to fifty dollars a week. It was not much. Many of the agents were not able to look away from bribes they were offered to let the buying and selling of alcohol continue.

The courts were quickly jam-packed with alcohol-related cases. They had been quite busy before Prohibition. Now the same number of judges had to get through thousands more cases each year. Before the law could send anyone to jail, they would first need to hold a trial by jury. The jury would decide if the person was guilty or not. The courts were too busy. They would never be able to hold enough trials. So the federal judges did their best. They made lawbreakers pay small fines. They had to throw out many cases. The lucky

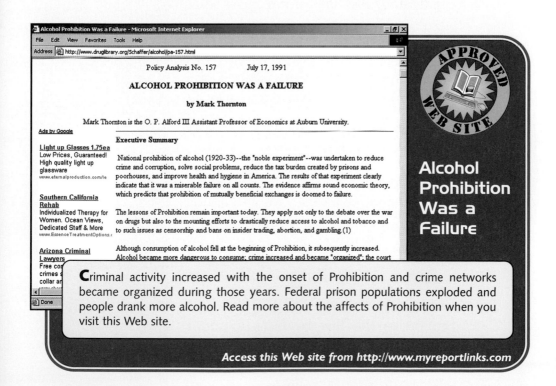

Criminal activity increased with the onset of Prohibition and crime networks became organized during those years. Federal prison populations exploded and people drank more alcohol. Read more about the affects of Prohibition when you visit this Web site.

Access this Web site from http://www.myreportlinks.com

defendants were off the hook. In 1929, federal courts threw out as many as seventy-five thousand cases. And that was just for one year![5]

→ CONGRESS WASHES THEIR HANDS

How much money was America willing to spend to enforce Prohibition? People were unsure how much it would cost. Wayne Wheeler of the Anti-Saloon League was optimistic. He said it would take around $5 million a year.[6] It quickly became clear that this was not enough. Much more money was needed. But where would the money come from? The government had less to spend now that they no longer received taxes from the liquor trade. Instead, they had to spend more money to police the illegal liquor trade. Congress did not seem very eager to spend any more money on Prohibition. In fact, they seemed glad to be rid of the issue. They had done their part in passing the amendment. Now they declared it a success. They refused to talk about it further. Many of them praised the strict laws in public. In private, they too broke the law by buying liquor from bootleggers.[7]

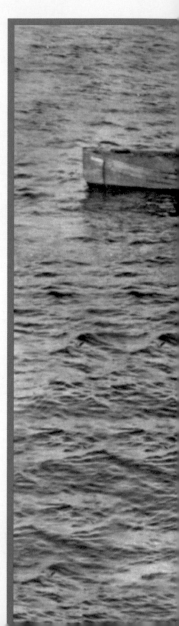

The wets were mad. The drys were mad. Letters flooded the White House. The law was not working. Crime was on the rise. Congress did not seem to care. They did not give the Prohibition Unit more money to uphold the law. Instead, they passed even more laws. More laws meant more work for the already stressed unit. President Warren

A rumrunner is out in the water, but a Coast Guard ship has pulled alongside of it. The bootlegging days of this rumrunner's crew are over.

G. Harding blamed the states. They were not doing their part. President Harding called on Americans to respect the law. He had been a lifelong drinker. Now he gave up it up in respect of the law.[8] Harding appointed a woman, Mabel Walker Willebrandt, as assistant attorney general. At the time, it was unusual for a woman to hold such a high public office. Her role was to see that the Volstead Act was upheld. It would not be an easy job.

⟳THE PROBLEM WITH CONCURRENT POWER

The states and the federal government had concurrent power. In other words, both were in charge of enforcing the Prohibition laws. The text of the Eighteenth Amendment said so. They would have to work together. Yet not all states were willing to help. Many did not have their own state laws to ban the sale of liquor. Other states had Prohibition laws, but they were not as strict as the Volstead Act. As a result, some states were not interested in sharing power. They did not want to spend their money to police a federal law. Why should they uphold a law that went against their local customs? A few states even rebelled against the Volstead Act. They passed their own laws that made beer with higher alcohol contents legal.[9] There seemed to be a battle brewing. Would the states or the federal government have the final say?

SPEAKEASIES, MOONSHINING, AND BOOTLEGGERS

In January 1920, the legal trade of alcohol was over and done for. The saloons closed down. Honest brewers and barkeepers found other work. The sale of liquor had brought in millions of dollars in profits each year. Now that money would be better spent elsewhere. Or would it? Also, it was against the law to make it or sell it, but it was not illegal to buy alcohol. Plenty of customers still wanted to buy it. It did not take long for people to see there was money to be made. One just had to be willing to break the law. Bootleggers were people who sold illegal liquor. One way they hid the alcohol was to stick a flask in the top of their boots. That was how they got the name "bootleggers."

Organized crime groups, such as the mafia, soon stepped in. They were already used to breaking the law. They were more than happy to reap the huge profits. They took control of the bootleggers and their markets. They saw a golden opportunity to get rich quickly. Often they could find a policeman who did not agree with the law. They paid him to look the other

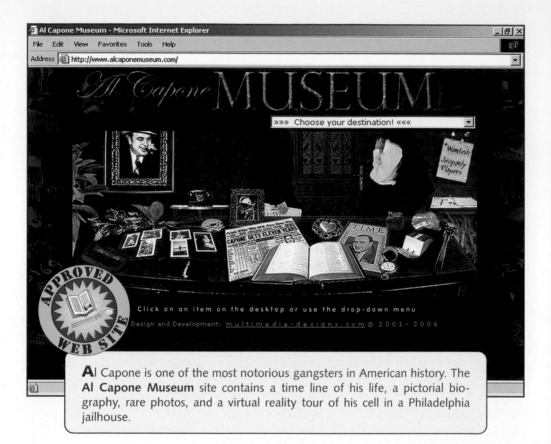

Al Capone Museum - Microsoft Internet Explorer

File   Edit   View   Favorites   Tools   Help

Address http://www.alcaponemuseum.com/

Al Capone MUSEUM

»»» Choose your destination! «««

Click on an item on the desktop or use the drop-down menu

Design and Development: multimedia-designs.com © 2001- 2006

Al Capone is one of the most notorious gangsters in American history. The **Al Capone Museum** site contains a time line of his life, a pictorial biography, rare photos, and a virtual reality tour of his cell in a Philadelphia jailhouse.

way while their men sold liquor. The crime bosses would pay a bribe to anyone who was willing to help them. They dealt harshly with anyone who dared to cross them.

⊖ CHICAGO'S SCARFACE

Probably the most infamous gangster of the Prohibition era was Al Capone. People called him Scarface. He had three slashes along his left cheek and neck. They were scars from a knife fight with a fellow gangster. Capone was the head of organized crime in Chicago. He became a wealthy man under Prohibition. He bribed the Chicago police to keep out of his way. He paid them nearly $30 million a year.[1] Al Capone said, "Prohibition is a business. All I do is supply a public demand."[2] However, the liquor trade was now a business without any rules. The government had no way to regulate it. It was now part of the seedy underworld of crime. Operating outside of the law, it was a violent field of work. Rival gangs were always at odds. They stole shipments of booze from each other. Gangsters carried machine guns

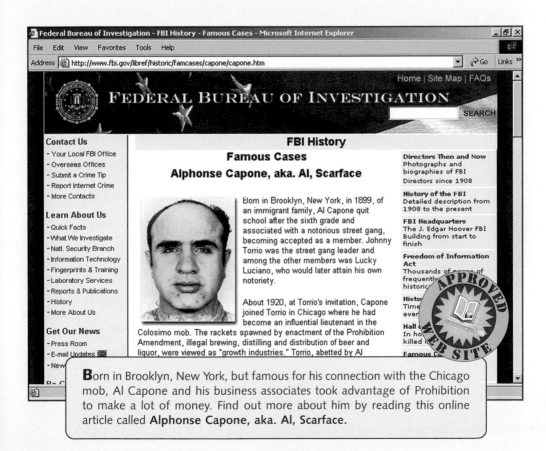

Born in Brooklyn, New York, but famous for his connection with the Chicago mob, Al Capone and his business associates took advantage of Prohibition to make a lot of money. Find out more about him by reading this online article called **Alphonse Capone, aka. Al, Scarface.**

and bombs, and they were not afraid to use them. It was a cutthroat business. In Chicago alone, hundreds of gangsters were killed during the 1920s. The nation's newspapers were full of headlines about shoot-outs between gangsters and police. It made for exciting news stories.

⊖SMUGGLING ON RUM ROW

Bootleggers sold liquor, but where did the liquor come from? One place it came from was boats along the coast. Liquor did not cost much at all in the Bahamas. Mexico, Barbados, Jamaica, Canada—there were many nearby places to buy it cheaply. Smugglers purchased as much as they could. They hid it in their boats. Then they brought it into the United States where they sold it for much more than they had bought it.

The United States has thousands of miles of shoreline. The Coast Guard patrols these waters. They make sure people do not smuggle illegal things into the country. However, there are only so many Coast Guard boats. They cannot be everywhere at once. One problem spot was Rum Row, off the coast of New York and New Jersey. Mother ships would dock miles offshore. They were filled to the hilt with illegal liquor. By staying miles off the coast, they avoided the Coast Guard. The Coast Guard only patrolled as far as three miles out. Smaller, speedier

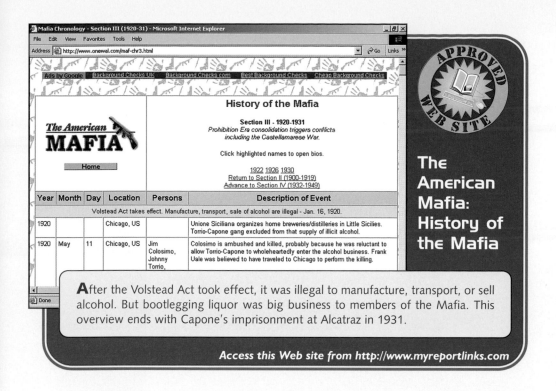

Mafia Chronology - Section III (1920-31) - Microsoft Internet Explorer

File   Edit   View   Favorites   Tools   Help

Address http://www.onewal.com/maf-chr3.html   Go   Links »

Ads by Google   Background Checks UK   Background Checks.com   Best Background Checks   Cheap Background Checks

The American MAFIA

Home

History of the Mafia

Section III - 1920-1931
*Prohibition Era consolidation triggers conflicts
including the Castellamarese War.*

Click highlighted names to open bios.

1922 1926 1930
Return to Section II (1900-1919)
Advance to Section IV (1932-1949)

Year	Month	Day	Location	Persons	Description of Event
					Volstead Act takes effect. Manufacture, transport, sale of alcohol are illegal - Jan. 16, 1920.
1920			Chicago, US		Unione Siciliana organizes home breweries/distilleries in Little Sicilies. Torrio-Capone gang excluded from that supply of illicit alcohol.
1920	May	11	Chicago, US	Jim Colosimo, Johnny Torrio,	Colosimo is ambushed and killed, probably because he was reluctant to allow Torrio-Capone to wholeheartedly enter the alcohol business. Frank Uale was believed to have traveled to Chicago to perform the killing.

Done

The American Mafia: History of the Mafia

After the Volstead Act took effect, it was illegal to manufacture, transport, or sell alcohol. But bootlegging liquor was big business to members of the Mafia. This overview ends with Capone's imprisonment at Alcatraz in 1931.

Access this Web site from http://www.myreportlinks.com

boats went out to meet the mother ships. They would bring the contraband ashore.

Bill McCoy was probably the most famous smuggler on Rum Row. Have you ever heard of the phrase "the real McCoy?" It means something that is genuine. Some people say that the phrase traces its origins back to McCoy the smuggler. People who bought rye whiskey and rum from McCoy knew they were getting the real thing.[3] McCoy outwitted the Coast Guard time and time again. He made a huge fortune. Eventually he was caught. A jury sentenced him to nine months in jail. After that, he gave up smuggling. Organized crime now controlled the rum running. There was no room for individual smugglers like McCoy.

→ MOONSHINE AND HOME BREW

Some people did not feel comfortable buying liquor from bootleggers. If they still wanted to drink, they made their own liquor at home. It was simple to do. They could buy a copper still at any hardware store. A still is a piece of equipment used to make liquor. A still only cost five dollars. The main ingredient in home-brewed liquor was corn sugar. It was very cheap and easy to buy. People could find a recipe at the public library. Most libraries had pamphlets about making alcohol from corn and other grains and fruits. The government itself had published them.[4] They had done so back in the days before Prohibition, of course. Now it was against the law to use a still. It was illegal even in the privacy of your own home. It was a risk that many were willing to take. The law did not seem to be enforceable. After all, there were only three thousand agents in the Prohibition Unit. They had to cover the entire nation. They were battling powerful

During Prohibition, many people resorted to making their own alcohol. One of these men is holding up a bottle of moonshine he filled illegally at their outdoor still.

crime bosses and rich bootleggers. It did not seem likely the agents would worry too much about private stills.

In the countryside, people made big batches of liquor. They called it "moonshine" because they made it by the light of the moon. In the dark of night, no one would see what they were up to. They sold it to bootleggers, who brought it to towns and cities. Moonshiners had big stills that they hid in the woods. They moved their operations every so often so the police would not find them. As a rule, they did not make much money. They were often poor people. There were not many jobs in rural areas. It was hard to make a living. Moonshiners often turned to making illegal alcohol as a last resort. It was the bootleggers who made the profits.

→ Blindness and Paralysis

Some bootleggers got their hands on industrial alcohol. It was not meant to be drunk. It had poisons in it. The law said that poisons had to be added. That way people would not drink it. Even so, some bootleggers sold it. Their customers did not know it was poisoned. The bootleggers boiled it down to get rid of some of the toxins. They filtered it and added water. Sometimes they put in dyes to change the color. The poisons made some people go blind. Others lost use of their legs. Thousands died after drinking it. In 1930, thousands of people lost use of their legs after drinking a poisoned drink called "jake." Jake stood for Jamaican ginger extract.[5]

Many Americans were horrified. Could it be that the government would rather poison its own people than allow them to take a drink? Was not the whole point of outlawing alcohol to rid society of a poison? Now people were drinking much more harmful poisons. This was not right. Still, not everyone felt this way. Yes, they did agree it was tragic that people had died. However, it would never have happened if they had not broken the law. They felt the lawbreakers got what they deserved.

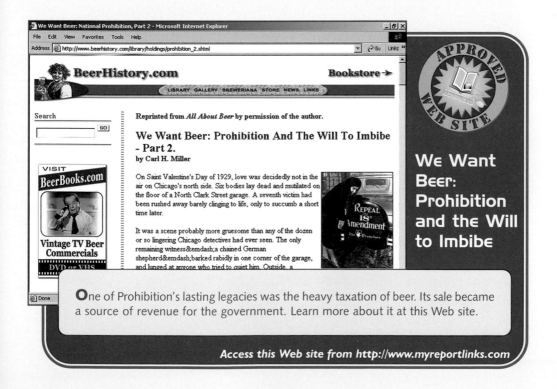

We Want Beer: Prohibition and the Will to Imbibe

One of Prohibition's lasting legacies was the heavy taxation of beer. Its sale became a source of revenue for the government. Learn more about it at this Web site.

Access this Web site from http://www.myreportlinks.com

➡NEAR BEER AND NEEDLE BEER

Not all breweries had shut down their operations.
They were still allowed to make a drink called
near beer. Near beer was beer that had very little
alcohol. It had less than one half of one percent
alcohol. To brew near beer, first they had to make
regular beer. Then they removed the alcohol. The
alcohol was supposed to be thrown away, but it
rarely was. It was worth a lot of money on the
black market. Bootleggers bought the alcohol.
They used a syringe to shoot the alcohol back into
the near beer. They called it needle beer.

➡WILLIS-CAMPBELL ACT OF 1921

Under the Prohibition laws, doctors could use
alcohol as medicine. It was legal for them to do so.
With a prescription, anyone could go to his or her
local pharmacy and buy liquor. People were eager
to get a prescription. There were plenty of corrupt
doctors and chemists who were willing to help
them. Once again, the risk did not seem very high.
There were 11 million prescriptions for alcohol
each and every year. Prohibition agents could
never sort through all of them. How would they
know which were for legitimate illnesses and
which were phony? The drys complained about
this loophole. Congress tried to put a stop to this
practice. They did not give any more money to
enforce the Volstead Act. Instead, they passed

another law—the Willis-Campbell Act. It came to be known as the Emergency Beer Act. The new law put many restrictions on doctors. The doctors were insulted and angry.[6] Did Congress know more about medicine than they did? What exactly gave Congress the right to tell them how to do their job?

⊖Speakeasies and Blind Pigs

For many Americans, it was part of their culture to drink alcohol. It was a tradition to drink in public. Now the saloons were gone. People still wanted to

Learn more about temperance and Prohibition from this informative article called **Alcohol, Temperance & Prohibition.** The types of propaganda commonly used by the antialcohol activists are discussed, including the use of religious pamphlets, posters, and songs.

EDITOR'S CHOICE

Deputy Commissioner John A. Leach of the New York City Police Department (right) looks on as agents pour confiscated liquor into the sewer.

drink in public. In the cities, speakeasies popped up to take the place of the saloons. It was important to "speak easy," or quietly, so no one would over-hear when you ordered a drink. It was not cheap to buy a drink at a speakeasy. Poor people could not afford it. In this way, speakeasies were very different from the saloons. They were for people with money, and as a result, they were more upscale than the filthy saloons. Some speakeasies were just a back room in a restaurant. You had to know the password to get in. Sometimes they were called "blind pigs" or "blind tigers." The bar-keeper sold tickets to see a "blind pig" he kept in the back room. If you bought a ticket, you also got a free drink. Of course, there was no blind pig.

→ Gin Fizzes and Highballs

Since it was legal to drink in your own house, peo-ple threw parties. Rich people would show off by serving expensive whiskey. If they could afford real whiskey at black market prices, they must have been very wealthy indeed. Cocktail parties were all the rage. Cocktails are a kind of drink. They consist of liquor mixed with other things like juice, ginger ale, or seltzer. They were popular during Prohibition because they covered up the awful taste of the homemade gin. The drinks had funny names like gin fizzes, lime rickeys, high-balls, and Manhattans.

This woman is dressed in the flapper style that was popular in the 1920s. In addition, she is hiding a flask of booze in her boot.

In Harlem, a part of New York City, rents were expensive in the 1920s. Jobs were scarce for the African Americans who lived there. When rent came due, sometimes there was no money to pay for it. One way people could raise money quickly was by throwing a big party. To get in, one paid a fee at the door. Inside the apartment, there were drinks for sale. Musicians played jazz music and everybody danced. The money from the party paid the next month's rent. It was a risky business, though. To make money, the people living there had to allow many people in, even people they did not know. There was always the risk that a paying guest was actually an undercover agent. The people who threw the parties could hardly afford to bribe police officers. Unlike the wealthier party throwers, they did not have the clout to complain to higher-ups. They were easy targets for any police who were trying to prove they were enforcing the law.[7]

➔FLAPPERS AND SHEIKS

People had a name for the decade of the 1920s. They called it the Roaring Twenties. Times were changing very fast. Young women no longer wore corsets and ankle-length skirts like their mothers had. Now it was the fashion to wear knee-length skirts and long strings of pearls. They went out in the evenings and danced a new dance called the

Charleston. Their dates wore their hair slicked back and parted straight down the middle. They drank cocktails. This new style of girl was called a flapper. The young men who went out with them were called sheiks. Before Prohibition, middle-class women rarely drank alcohol in public. It was just not done. Saloons were for men. Now that drinking was against the law, it had become in vogue for women to drink. Young men and women now drank together.[8] These young people seemed out of control to older folks. Many were shocked by their wild ways. Some people blamed Prohibition for a new era of lawlessness. What did it mean for the future of the United States?

5 PROHIBITION IN THE COURTS

The men who wrote the U.S. Constitution had high hopes for their young country. They thought long and hard about the kind of government that would be best. They wanted to create a government that would represent the will of the people. To make sure that would be the case, the founding fathers did a wise thing. They split up the government into parts. They made three different branches. The three branches share the power. They watch over each other. They make sure one branch does not grow too powerful. It is a very smart system of checks and balances.

What are the three branches? First there is the executive branch. That is the office of the president. People vote for the president every four years. The president and the members of his executive departments ensure people follow the laws of the land. Second is the legislative branch. That is the United States Congress. The Congress is made up of two houses. These are the Senate and the House of Representatives.

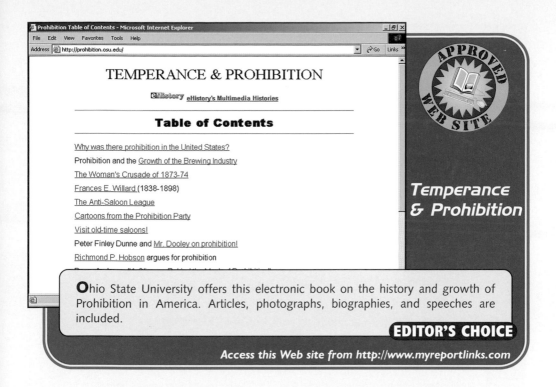

TEMPERANCE & PROHIBITION

eHistory eHistory's Multimedia Histories

Table of Contents

Why was there prohibition in the United States?
Prohibition and the Growth of the Brewing Industry
The Woman's Crusade of 1873-74
Frances E. Willard (1838-1898)
The Anti-Saloon League
Cartoons from the Prohibition Party
Visit old-time saloons!
Peter Finley Dunne and Mr. Dooley on prohibition!
Richmond P. Hobson argues for prohibition

Ohio State University offers this electronic book on the history and growth of Prohibition in America. Articles, photographs, biographies, and speeches are included.

EDITOR'S CHOICE

Access this Web site from http://www.myreportlinks.com

They make the laws. The judicial branch is the third. This branch is the federal courts. The highest court in the United States is the Supreme Court. It makes decisions about laws that have to do with the Constitution. The Supreme Court has the final say.

⊝The Three Branches in Action

Thanks in large part to Congress, the Eighteenth Amendment was the law. It was a law they later did little to support. After it had passed, Congress dropped it like a hot potato. Each year Congress agrees on a budget. They decide how much money each government agency will have to spend for

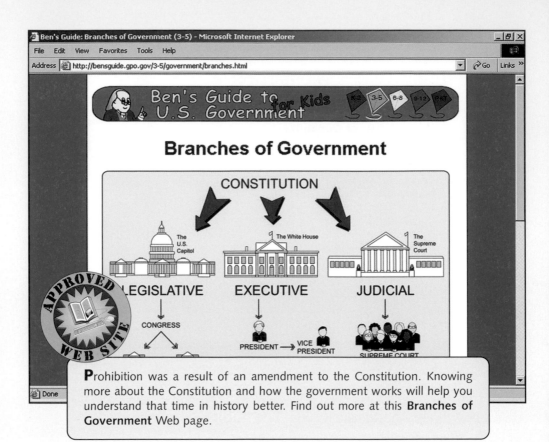

Ben's Guide: Branches of Government (3-5) - Microsoft Internet Explorer

File   Edit   View   Favorites   Tools   Help

Address http://bensguide.gpo.gov/3-5/government/branches.html   Go   Links »

Ben's Guide to U.S. Government for Kids   K-2 3-5 6-8 9-12 P&T

Branches of Government

CONSTITUTION

The U.S. Capitol   The White House   The Supreme Court

LEGISLATIVE   EXECUTIVE   JUDICIAL

CONGRESS   PRESIDENT → VICE PRESIDENT   SUPREME COURT

Done

Prohibition was a result of an amendment to the Constitution. Knowing more about the Constitution and how the government works will help you understand that time in history better. Find out more at this **Branches of Government** Web page.

the year. They had a lot to say about the benefits of Prohibition. When it came time to allocate the money, the talk died down. They never gave the Prohibition Unit enough funds.[1] With such a lack of money, the agents' hands were tied. They could never hope to do their job right. The unit was in a tough spot. No matter how hard the agents worked, they could never hope to enforce the law.

What about the executive branch, that of the president? As the leader of the country, the president is in charge. He sees that people obey the law.

Yet the presidents in power during Prohibition did not step up to the plate. President Woodrow Wilson was in office when the Eighteenth Amendment passed. He did not agree with it. Still, he did little to stop it from becoming part of the Constitution. His health was failing. The next president was Warren G. Harding. Harding was fond of drink himself. Despite the law, for a while he kept right on drinking. He was hardly a good example for the country to follow. Eventually he did quit drinking, but he died soon after. His vice president, Calvin Coolidge, took over upon his death. Coolidge was not a drinker. He came from a strict and upright New England family. People thought he would do a good job with Prohibition. Coolidge had no more success than Harding had. He blamed the states for not cooperating.[2] In 1928, Herbert Hoover won the election. He, too, spoke out strongly on the issue. He said citizens had a duty to obey the law. Hoover soon found that words were not enough. The problems of Prohibition continued to loom large.

⮕CHIEF JUSTICE TAFT

Two branches of the government were not doing their part to uphold the law. This did not include the judicial branch—it stood strong on the side of the law. At least the Supreme Court could say it did. This was due to a man named William Howard

This classic image depicts Georgia Congressman William D. Upshaw holding an umbrella over his head with the Capitol building in the background. The umbrella symbolized that he was a Dry.

Taft. Taft, a former president, was the Chief Justice of the Supreme Court from 1921 to 1930. He had not been a supporter of Prohibition before it passed. He did not think it belonged in the Constitution. That changed when it became a law. Then Taft became a staunch supporter. He believed in upholding the law to the letter.[3]

THE SUPREME COURT TAKES A STAND

Some people said the amendment went too far. Was it right for the government to police what one had to drink? Opponents of the law did not think so. They felt it went against their right to live a free life. The Constitution has a Bill of Rights. The Bill of Rights is there to protect Americans' personal freedoms. How could the Constitution protect freedom and, at the same time, control such a personal issue? Some people did not think the amendment was legal. It went against the Bill of Rights. They took their concerns to the courts.

Elihu Root was one of the best lawyers of the time. He had grave concerns about the amendment.[4] Feigenspan, a brewing company from New Jersey, wanted to hire Root. The company's owners thought the amendment was unconstitutional. He agreed to argue their case before the Supreme Court. People paid close attention to what Root had to say. He was a well-known figure in Washington. Root had served his country as secretary of

Elihu Root was a prominent lawyer and politician at the turn of the twentieth century. In 1920, he was unsuccessful in his bid to get the Supreme Court to decide that the Eighteenth Amendment was unconstitutional.

war and secretary of state. He had served as a United States senator. Root said that the amendment weakened the rights of the states. What about the states that did not agree with Prohibition? Why should they have to enforce a federal law? Root spoke with passion. However, the justices were not moved. In the summer of 1920, the Supreme Court took a stand. It ruled on seven cases, including Feigenspan's. Each of the cases had to do with the Eighteenth Amendment. The press called them the National Prohibition Cases. The ruling firmly backed up both the amendment and the Volstead Act. It brushed aside all the objections. It seemed that Prohibition was here to stay.

➡ *HAWKE V. SMITH* (1920)

Many folks in Ohio were not happy about Prohibition, even though Ohio had been one of the states that voted for the amendment. Enough people in the state were outraged that they held a state referendum on Prohibition. The citizens went to the polls and took a vote on the issue. A referendum is a good way to find out what the people want. The results came in. Ohioans had spoken. They did not want Prohibition.

The people had voted to repeal the amendment. They did not win by much. Less than five hundred votes made the difference.[5] In the end, it was a wasted effort. The Supreme Court struck the referendum down. In the case *Hawke* v. *Smith* the Court ruled that the ratification had been valid. It could not be overturned. The Eighteenth Amendment stood, no matter what the people of the state might want.

⊖ *UNITED STATES* V. *LANZA* (1922)

The phrase "concurrent power" was causing a lot of confusion. The Supreme Court tried to clear some of this up in *United States* v. *Lanza*. Vito Lanza had been caught making liquor in Washington State. The state charged him with breaking state law. A

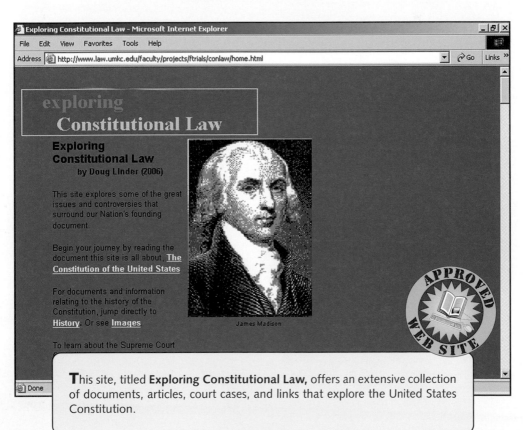

This site, titled **Exploring Constitutional Law,** offers an extensive collection of documents, articles, court cases, and links that explore the United States Constitution.

jury found him guilty. Then Lanza was charged a second time for the exact same crime. The federal government tried him for breaking the Eighteenth Amendment. They tried him in a federal court. In the United States, double jeopardy is against the law. That means a person cannot face more than

The Washington, D.C., police chased down this car driven by bootleggers on the streets of the nation's capital.

one trial for the same crime. It is guaranteed in the Bill of Rights. Lanza took his case to the Supreme Court. The Court ruled against Lanza. It said that people who broke the law by selling or making alcohol could face trial twice. They could be tried in a federal court and again in a state court for the same crime. How could that be? The Constitution only applied to federal courts. It did not affect the states. The states also had the right to prosecute those who broke state laws. The Court seemed to be defending the rights of the states.

➔THE CARROLL DECISION (1925)

Federal agents in Michigan pulled over a car. They suspected that the owner, George Carroll, was a bootlegger. The agents searched the car thoroughly. Sure enough, behind the cushions, they found many bottles of liquor. When the case came to trial, Carroll's lawyers complained. They said the police had no right to search the car. They did not have a warrant. A

81

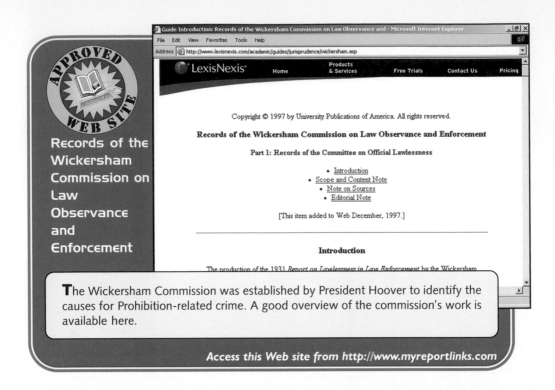

Records of the Wickersham Commission on Law Observance and Enforcement

Part 1: Records of the Committee on Official Lawlessness

- Introduction
- Scope and Content Note
- Note on Sources
- Editorial Note

[This item added to Web December, 1997.]

Introduction

The production of the 1931 *Report on Lawlessness in Law Enforcement* by the Wickersham

Records of the Wickersham Commission on Law Observance and Enforcement

The Wickersham Commission was established by President Hoover to identify the causes for Prohibition-related crime. A good overview of the commission's work is available here.

Access this Web site from http://www.myreportlinks.com

warrant is a document from a judge. It states what the police are searching for. The police said it would take too long to get a warrant. The car would have been miles away by the time the police had obtained the warrant. They thought Carroll might be a bootlegger. That was enough to justify a search. The Supreme Court agreed with the police. Police could search a car. They did not need a permit. It was a blow to bootleggers. The Supreme Court was doing its part to crack down on crime.

→ OLMSTEAD V. UNITED STATES (1928)

Prohibition had been the law for eight years. It was true that alcohol consumption had gone down. Yet it had not gone away.[6] Crime was on the rise and the police were losing the battle. They needed some new weapons. One idea they had was wiretapping. They secretly listened in to private phone calls. They caught one bootlegger, Roy Olmstead, by listening to his telephone calls. Olmstead's lawyers argued that wiretapping was a kind of search, therefore the police needed a warrant. The case went to the Supreme Court. They ruled in favor of the police. Americans started to grow worried. They could see they were losing personal freedoms. Now police could stop and search their cars on a whim. They could be listening in on private phone calls. What was next?

THE WICKERSHAM COMMISSION

President Hoover saw that crime was on the rise. He knew it was a problem that was not going away. Something had to be done. He put together a team of people: the National Commission on Law Observance and Enforcement. He asked them to examine the issue. They were to do some research and write a report. They were to suggest how to make things better. Hoover hoped that they could find a way to solve the problems of Prohibition.

George W. Wickersham led the group. He was a lawyer from New York. He and his group published a full report in 1931. They had found many

Hooch hounds such as this one were trained to smell alcohol so that agents could catch bootleggers and other people illegally carrying liquor.

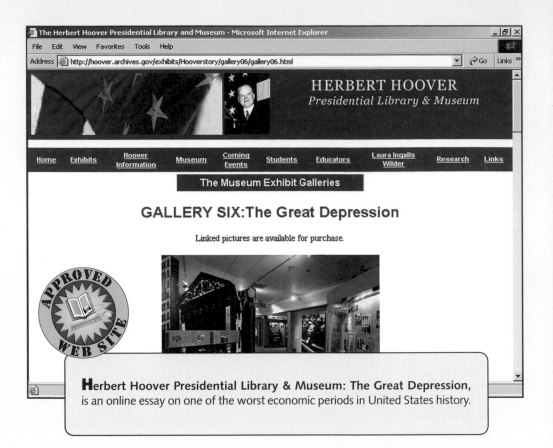

The Herbert Hoover Presidential Library and Museum - Microsoft Internet Explorer

File Edit View Favorites Tools Help

Address http://hoover.archives.gov/exhibits/Hooverstory/gallery06/gallery06.html Go Links »

HERBERT HOOVER
Presidential Library & Museum

Home   Exhibits   Hoover Information   Museum   Coming Events   Students   Educators   Laura Ingalls Wilder   Research   Links

The Museum Exhibit Galleries

GALLERY SIX: The Great Depression

Linked pictures are available for purchase.

Herbert Hoover Presidential Library & Museum: The Great Depression, is an online essay on one of the worst economic periods in United States history.

problems. To start with, the public did not think very highly of the Eighteenth Amendment. They did not respect the law. This was also true for many public officials. They were the people in charge of enforcing the law! There was also a lack of funding to enforce the law. The risks of breaking the law were outweighed by the money to be made. Bootleggers were raking in huge profits. The Wickersham group found that Prohibition was impossible to enforce. Still, they did not suggest that the law be repealed.

→ THE TIDE BEGINS TO TURN

In 1920, the United States took a head count. They used a type of survey called a census. A census counts how many people there are living in a certain area. It also shows where people live. The results of the census showed something interesting. In the past, most Americans lived in the countryside. This was no longer true. Now more people lived in large towns and cities. That was a big change. The government would need to adjust. They had to accommodate this change. They had to fix the congressional districts. The districts were drawn based on an old census. Because the districts were old, city dwellers did not have enough representatives in Congress. Rural people had too many. That was not fair. So they redrew the congressional districts in 1929. Suddenly, city people had more of a voice in Washington. Prohibition had never been popular in the cities. Now there was less support in Congress for Prohibition.

Not long after that blow, Prohibition suffered another hit. It lost a friend in the Supreme Court. In 1930, Chief Justice William Howard Taft died. Taft had been a conservative. Time and time again, he had led the Court to uphold the Eighteenth Amendment. He supported the police in their efforts to enforce it. Taft's successor was Charles Evan Hughes. Hughes brought a new mind-set to the bench. The Court turned its focus to protecting the rights of individuals.[7]

→ AMERICA COMES CRASHING DOWN

The Roaring Twenties was a time of success. The American economy was at an all-time high. It was too good to last. In October 1929, the stock market crashed. Banks lost their money and had to close their doors. In those days, bank accounts were not insured like they are today. People lost all the money they had saved. Millions were out of work. There were no jobs to be had. Suddenly people were worried about basic needs. Where would they find food for their families? It cast a new light on the woes of Prohibition. Why should organized crime make all the profits from the liquor trade? If alcohol were legal, there would be more jobs and less crime. The government could be taking in taxes from the liquor trade.[8] America was spending so much money on law enforcement. Would the money not be better spent to keep people from starving?

THE END OF A NOBLE EXPERIMENT 6

The Eighteenth Amendment had enjoyed wide support at first. Very few people had spoken out to oppose it. The country seemed to agree that a ban on liquor was the right thing to do. Of course, there had been a few groups who tried to block it. They were people who would lose money if a ban went into effect.

Then the nation tried to live under the Eighteenth Amendment. Soon the ban no longer seemed like such a good idea. More and more, people spoke out against the law. The opposition grew and grew. It now included people from all walks of life. Some folks thought the federal government was out of line. It had grown too powerful. What about the states' rights? And the rise in crime was fearful. Why should the crime bosses be millionaires while there was a lack of honest jobs? Then there was the police. Their powers were growing every day. They needed to be strong to fight organized crime. But what about the rights of law-abiding citizens? Was it right that they had to give up freedoms so that Prohibition could be enforced?

John Phillip Hill, a Congressman from Maryland, pours water onto a globe to show his support for the Wets.

→ THE OPPOSITION GROWS

Captain William H. Stayton was one man who had dared to speak up right from the start. He did not speak out because he stood to lose money. He spoke out because he was sure that Prohibition was wrong. Stayton had been an officer in the Navy. It was clear that he cared about his country. People saw that and respected his point of view. He did not think that the government had the right to tell the states what to do. He felt that the Eighteenth Amendment got in the way of the American way of life. In America, people have the right to govern themselves. For it to work, people must have control at a local level. Stayton thought this was vital. He was sure that the Eighteenth Amendment would take away local control.[1]

Stayton and his friends formed a group in 1919. They tried to convince congressmen not to vote for the Eighteenth Amendment. They called themselves the Association against the Prohibition Amendment. They were not brewers, nor distillers, nor saloon keepers. They were upstanding citizens. But it was too little and too late. Stayton was disappointed when the amendment became law. Yet he did not give up. His group kept speaking out against Prohibition and their membership grew.

Even some people who had once backed the amendment changed their minds. They now worked just as hard to reverse the ban. Pauline

Sabin of Chicago was one of these people. She said, "I was one of the women who favored prohibition . . . but I am now convinced it has proved a failure."[2] Women had worked so hard to ban alcohol. They had thought that they were protecting their families from liquor. That dream had never come true. Both women and men were fed up with the problems of Prohibition. And now women had more of a say in the matter. They could make a difference by voting. In 1920, the Twentieth Amendment passed. It gave women the right to vote. With their new power, some women chose to speak up against the ban on liquor. Sabin and others formed a new group: the Women's Organization for National Prohibition Reform.

As Unlikely as a Hummingbird on Mars

All of the groups who opposed Prohibition wanted to see a change in the law. Many of them wanted to be rid of the Eighteenth Amendment once and for all. There was only one way to strike down the amendment. That was to repeal it. It had never been done before. They would need to pass another constitutional amendment to do so. It would need the support of two thirds of the House and Senate. Then thirty-six states would have to vote for it. No, it did not seem very likely. Senator Morris Sheppard was the man who had first introduced the bill in the Senate. He was confident that

Chicago had its share of troubles in the 1920s. Racial tensions, police corruption, crime, and gangsters were just some of them. Find out more when you read the **Chicago in the Roaring Twenties** article from Roosevelt University.

repeal could not happen. He went so far as to say it could not be done. "There is as much chance of repealing the Eighteenth Amendment as there is for a humming-bird to fly to the planet Mars with the Washington Monument tied to its tail," he boasted.[3] Prohibition was firmly embedded in the Constitution. It appeared to be a law that was here to stay.

➔ WHAT TO DO?

Most everyone agreed that Prohibition was not working. Some people said it just needed more

One of the problems that Prohibition agents faced was that many Americans still wanted to drink. This is an image of a warehouse filled with confiscated booze.

time. When the Great Depression hit, this way of thinking lost steam. The problems of Prohibition were not going away. What were the options? Americans could just ignore the law, but that did not seem like a good solution. If people did not obey one law, all the laws might lose their strength. Most people agreed that lawlessness was not the answer. If the government spent lots of money, they might be able to enforce the law better. It would mean more police, more courts, and more jails. It would mean more searches and wiretapping. It also would mean less freedom. Americans are proud to live in a free country. This did not seem like the best solution. Some people suggested that they could just change the law a bit. If it were less strict, maybe people would obey it. Maybe beer and wine could be allowed. But the Eighteenth Amendment was quite clear. It outlawed any "intoxicating beverage." That meant beer and wine. The last option was to repeal the law. If Congress passed an amendment to repeal the law, then it would go back to the states to decide.

→ FRANKLIN D. ROOSEVELT AND THE DEMOCRATS

In 1932, Americans went to the polls to elect a new president. Four years earlier, President Herbert Hoover had won. He was a Republican. He had run as a dry candidate. He had made a promise that he would enforce Prohibition. He had called

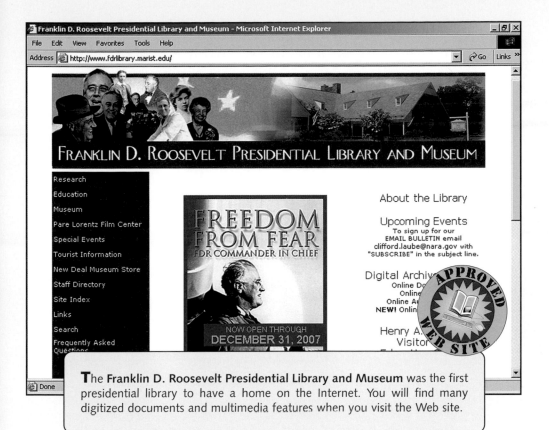

The **Franklin D. Roosevelt Presidential Library and Museum** was the first presidential library to have a home on the Internet. You will find many digitized documents and multimedia features when you visit the Web site.

Prohibition "a great social and economic experiment, noble in motive and far-reaching in purpose."[4] At the time, the Republicans had claimed credit for the strong economy. It was at an all-time high when Hoover took office. Then the stock market crashed. Times were hard. Many people pinned the blame on Hoover. They thought he should have seen what was coming. As the old saying goes, "what goes up must come down." Hoover ran for president again. He changed his stand on Prohibition. He now thought it should be sent back to the states. The states should decide whether repeal was a good idea. That made his dry supporters unhappy. Yet the wets were not ready to support Hoover, either. Many voters looked for a new face to fix the problems of the Depression.

That new face was Franklin D. Roosevelt. Roosevelt was the governor of New York. He ran on the Democratic ticket and won the election. The Democratic Party had played second fiddle in Washington for nearly one hundred years. Now the party gained prestige. A lot of their support was due to their stance on Prohibition.[5] They made repeal of the Eighteenth Amendment part of the party platform. The Democrats also won seats in Congress. They held a majority in both the House and the Senate. Americans had spoken. Prohibition must go! Suddenly many of the old lawmakers who had supported Prohibition were gone. Some were still there, but now they were in the minority. They did not have enough votes to pass or defeat a bill.

➲THE TWENTY-FIRST AMENDMENT

Congress felt it had a mandate from the people. Americans were sick and tired of the ban on liquor. The results of the election had made that much clear. They wasted no time. They did not even wait for Roosevelt to take office. Senator John J. Blaine of Wisconsin brought a bill to the floor of the Senate. He proposed to add the Twenty-first Amendment to the Constitution. The new amendment had three parts. The first section would end Prohibition. It stated that the Eighteenth Amendment was repealed. Alcohol, in all its forms, would be legal once again. The second part addressed the transport of alcohol between the states. It agreed to support the states. It made it against federal law to bring alcohol into a state, if that state had laws against it. The third part of the amendment said that the people, not the state legislatures, must vote to ratify the amendment.

The Constitution says there are two ways to ratify an amendment. The first is through the state

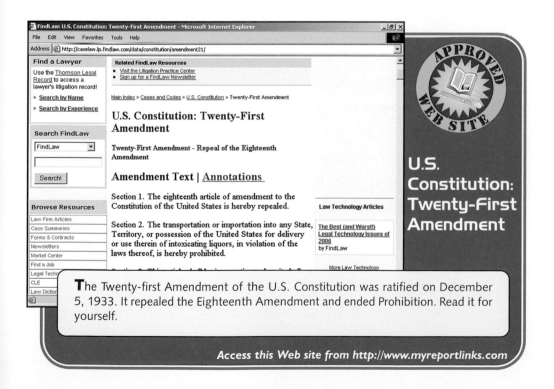

The Twenty-first Amendment of the U.S. Constitution was ratified on December 5, 1933. It repealed the Eighteenth Amendment and ended Prohibition. Read it for yourself.

Access this Web site from http://www.myreportlinks.com

legislatures. That is how the Eighteenth Amendment was passed. In fact, that is how all the amendments to date had been passed. The Twenty-first Amendment was to be different. Wets were worried that the state legislatures would still be full of dry votes. So they insisted that the issue be put before the citizens of the states. The citizens would go to the polls to vote. They would choose between wet and dry delegates. The delegates would then meet at a statewide convention. They would cast their votes for or against the proposed amendment.

THE AMENDMENT IS PASSED

Now the wet Democrats were in control in Washington. The bill easily passed in the Senate. The vote was sixty-three for the bill and twenty-three against. It passed with flying colors in the House. There were 289 votes for, and 121 votes against. On February 20, Congress sent the bill to the states. Now the people would have their say. The states were also eager to act. They organized conventions. Michigan was the first state to take a vote. Out of a hundred people, only a single person voted against it. In the next few months, many states followed suit. Only one, North Carolina, voted against repeal. On December 5, 1933, Utah held a vote. The state's delegates wanted to be the thirty-sixth state to approve it. Then they could say they had made the Twenty-first Amendment a law. They were worried that Maine might beat them to it.[6] So, without any debate, they took a vote. The roll call vote was broadcast over the radio across the nation. The Twenty-first Amendment had passed. It was unlikely and against the odds that it had happened. The states had ratified the Eighteenth Amendment in a little over a year. The repeal now happened just as quickly. It had taken the states only ten months to ratify the Twenty-first Amendment.

The new amendment struck down the Eighteenth Amendment. It made it null and void. It was almost as if Congress had never written it. It gave full power back to the states. If a state wanted to have laws about alcohol use, then that was fine. The federal government would not make laws on the issue. It was not a good idea to make such laws for the entire country to follow. America had learned that the hard way.

→ LESSONS FOR TODAY

If you read the Constitution today, you will still see the Eighteenth Amendment. A law may be changed and then forgotten over time. This is not the case with amendments. They will always remain a part of our Constitution. Why did the Eighteenth Amendment fail? What made it different from other changes to the Constitution? There

These women are enjoying a glass of wine and some conversation at a bar restaurant. Since 1933, alcohol has legally been a part of America's social fabric.

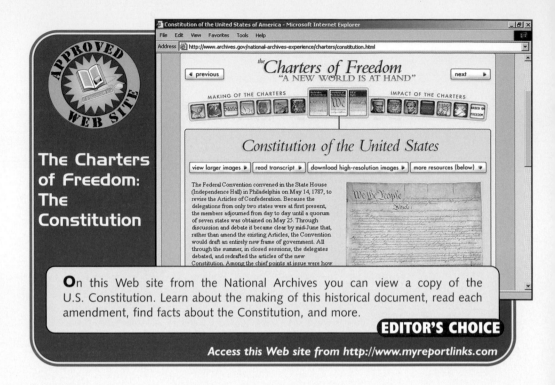

The Charters of Freedom: The Constitution

Constitution of the United States of America - Microsoft Internet Explorer

File   Edit   View   Favorites   Tools   Help

Address http://www.archives.gov/national-archives-experience/charters/constitution.html

the Charters of Freedom
"A NEW WORLD IS AT HAND"

◄ previous   next ►

MAKING OF THE CHARTERS   IMPACT OF THE CHARTERS

Constitution of the United States

view larger images ►   read transcript ►   download high-resolution images ►   more resources (below) ▼

The Federal Convention convened in the State House
(Independence Hall) in Philadelphia on May 14, 1787, to
revise the Articles of Confederation. Because the
delegations from only two states were at first present,
the members adjourned from day to day until a quorum
of seven states was obtained on May 25. Through
discussion and debate it became clear by mid-June that,
rather than amend the existing Articles, the Convention
would draft an entirely new frame of government. All
through the summer, in closed sessions, the delegates
debated, and redrafted the articles of the new
Constitution. Among the chief points at issue were how

On this Web site from the National Archives you can view a copy of the U.S. Constitution. Learn about the making of this historical document, read each amendment, find facts about the Constitution, and more.

EDITOR'S CHOICE

Access this Web site from http://www.myreportlinks.com

were a few things. First of all, it was the only amendment that tried to improve moral conduct of the nation. In other words, it told people how they could act. Not everyone agreed with this code of behavior. For a law to work, it must have the support of the citizens. A second reason was that it took away from the freedom of Americans. It took away people's right to make a personal decision. It tried to dictate what people could drink.

The Eighteenth Amendment is the only amendment to have been repealed. The Constitution is not easy to change. An amendment requires a lot of support from many different groups of people. The Eighteenth Amendment was repealed within fourteen years. It just goes to show how quickly the ideas of a nation can change.

THE EFFORT TO LEGALIZE MARIJUANA

Banning liquor did not get rid of the Demon Rum. Everyone saw that it did not work. It is interesting, then, that the United States does still ban other drugs. In recent years, there has been a push to lift the ban on one drug. Marijuana comes from the leaves of a plant. Its proponents say it is not a dangerous drug. They argue that it can help people who are suffering from pain. They say it is not as addictive as alcohol or tobacco.[7] In twelve states, the people agree. They have passed laws on the issue. It is legal to use marijuana with a doctors prescription, if one needs it as medicine. To date, the United States federal government does not agree with these laws. The Supreme Court recently ruled on the matter in *Gonzalez v. Raich*. The Court supported the federal Drug Enforcement Agency (DEA). It said the DEA has every right to prosecute people who use marijuana. They have the right, even if the state does not agree.

ALCOHOL: A LEGAL DRUG

Alcohol is a kind of drug. It is a drug that has been around for a long time. It is a drug that many people in the United States use. In some cultures, people have a daily drink at dinner time. Liquor is often

Although there are some benefits to imbibing alcohol, many suffer from alcoholism and heavy drinking.

served at parties and weddings. Some doctors today say that a glass of wine a day can be good for adults. They believe it helps keep the heart healthy.[8] Doctors also warn against the dangers of alcohol abuse. People who drink a lot do serious damage to their bodies. Alcohol abuse can destroy the liver and cause liver cirrhosis. Today, liver cirrhosis is on the list of the top ten leading causes of death in America.

Like all drugs, alcohol can be dangerous. It causes many problems in America. People who are drunk are more likely to break the law. Drunken people commit 40 percent of all crimes.[9] Drinking and then climbing behind the wheel of a car can be deadly. Alcohol affects the brain. It leaves people slow to react. These people put themselves and innocent people in grave danger. In one year alone, 16,694 people died in alcohol-related car crashes in the United States.[10]

Prohibition may have failed. That does not mean there were not good reasons to try it in the first place. There are many problems with alcohol. They have not gone away. They still plague America. We will need to address these problems if they are to get better. Politicians are not eager to try again to solve the problems with laws. Who can blame them?

107

The Constitution of the United States

The text of the Constitution is presented here. All words are given their modern spelling and capitalization. Brackets [ ] indicate parts that have been changed or set aside by amendments.

Preamble

We the People of the United States, in Order to form a more perfect Union, establish Justice, insure domestic Tranquillity, provide for the common defence, promote the general Welfare, and secure the Blessings of Liberty to ourselves and our Posterity, do ordain and establish this Constitution for the United States of America.

Article I
The Legislative Branch

Section 1. All legislative powers herein granted shall be vested in a Congress of the United States, which shall consist of a Senate and House of Representatives.

The House of Representatives

Section 2. The House of Representatives shall be composed of members chosen every second year by the people of the several states, and the electors in each state shall have the qualifications requisite for electors of the most numerous branch of the state legislature.

No person shall be a Representative who shall not have attained to the age of twenty five years, and been seven years a citizen of the United States, and who shall not, when elected, be an inhabitant of that state in which he shall be chosen.

Representatives and direct taxes shall be apportioned among the several states which may be included within this union, according to their respective numbers, [which shall be determined by adding to the whole number of free persons, including those bound to service for a term of years, and excluding Indians not taxed, three fifth of all other persons]. The actual Enumeration shall be made within three years after the first meeting of the Congress of the United States, and within every subsequent term of ten years, in such manner as they shall by law direct. The number of Representatives shall not exceed one for every thirty thousand, but each state shall have at least one Representative; [and until such enumeration shall be made, the state of New Hampshire shall be entitled to chuse three, Massachusetts eight, Rhode Island and Providence Plantations one, Connecticut five, New York six, New Jersey four, Pennsylvania eight, Delaware one, Maryland six, Virginia ten, North Carolina five, South Carolina five, and Georgia three].

When vacancies happen in the Representation from any state, the executive authority thereof shall issue writs of election to fill such vacancies.

The House of Representatives shall choose their speaker and other officers; and shall have the sole power of impeachment.

The Senate

Section 3. The Senate of the United States shall be composed of two Senators from each state, [chosen by the legislature thereof,] for six years; and each Senator shall have one vote.

Immediately after they shall be assembled in consequence of the first election, they shall be divided as equally as may be into three classes. The seats of the Senators of the first class shall be vacated at the expiration of the second year, of the second class at the expiration of the fourth year, and the third class at the expiration of the sixth year, so that one third may be chosen every second year; [and if vacancies happen by resignation, or otherwise, during the recess of the legislature of any state, the executive thereof may make temporary appointments until the next meeting of the legislature, which shall then fill such vacancies].

No person shall be a Senator who shall not have attained to the age of thirty years, and been nine years a citizen of the United States and who shall not, when elected, be an inhabitant of that state for which he shall be chosen.

The Vice President of the United States shall be President of the Senate, but shall have no vote, unless they be equally divided.

The Senate shall choose their other officers, and also a President pro tempore, in the absence of the Vice President, or when he shall exercise the office of President of the United States.

The Senate shall have the sole power to try all impeachments. When sitting for that purpose, they shall be on oath or affirmation. When the President of the United States is tried, the Chief Justice shall preside: And no person shall be convicted without the concurrence of two thirds of the members present.

Judgment in cases of impeachment shall not extend further than to removal from office, and disqualification to hold and enjoy any office of honor, trust or profit under the United States: but the party convicted shall nevertheless be liable and subject to indictment, trial, judgment and punishment, according to law.

Organization of Congress

Section 4. The times, places and manner of holding elections for Senators and Representatives, shall be prescribed in each state by the legislature thereof; but the Congress may at any time by law make or alter such regulations, [except as to the places of choosing senators].

The Congress shall assemble at least once in every year, [and such meeting shall be on the first Monday in December], unless they shall by law appoint a different day.

Section 5. Each House shall be the judge of the elections, returns and qualifications of its own members, and a majority of each shall constitute a quorum to do business; but a smaller number may adjourn from day to day, and may be authorized to compel the attendance of absent members, in such manner, and under such penalties as each House may provide.

Each House may determine the rules of its proceedings, punish its members for disorderly behavior, and, with the concurrence of two thirds, expel a member.

Each House shall keep a journal of its proceedings, and from time to time publish the same, excepting such parts as may in their judgment require secrecy; and the yeas and nays of the members of either House on any question shall, at the desire of one fifth of those present, be entered on the journal.

Neither House, during the session of Congress, shall, without the consent of the other, adjourn for more than three days, nor to any other place than that in which the two Houses shall be sitting.

Section 6. The Senators and Representatives shall receive a compensation for their services, to be ascertained by law, and paid out of the treasury of the United States. They shall in all cases, except treason, felony and breach of the peace, be privileged from arrest during their attendance at the session of their respective Houses, and in going to and returning from the same; and for any speech or debate in either House, they shall not be questioned in any other place.

No Senator or Representative shall, during the time for which he was elected, be appointed to any civil office under the authority of the United States, which shall have been created, or the emoluments whereof shall have been increased during such time: and no person holding any office under the United States, shall be a member of either House during his continuance in office.

Section 7. All bills for raising revenue shall originate in the House of Representatives; but the Senate may propose or concur with amendments as on other Bills.

Every bill which shall have passed the House of Representatives and the Senate, shall, before it become a law, be presented to the President of the United States; if he approve he shall sign it, but if not he shall return it, with his objections to that House in which it shall have originated, who shall enter the objections at large on their journal, and proceed to reconsider it. If after such reconsideration two thirds of that House shall agree to pass the bill, it shall be sent, together with the objections, to the other House, by which it shall likewise be reconsidered, and if approved by two thirds of that House, it shall become a law. But in all such cases the votes of both Houses shall be determined by yeas and nays, and the names of the persons voting for and against the bill shall be entered on the journal of each House respectively. If any bill shall not be returned by the President within ten days (Sundays excepted) after it shall have been presented to him, the same shall be a law, in like manner as if he had signed it, unless the Congress by their adjournment prevent its return, in which case it shall not be a law.

Every order, resolution, or vote to which the concurrence of the Senate and House of Representatives may be necessary (except on a question of adjournment) shall be presented to the President of the United States; and before the same shall take effect, shall be approved by him, or being disapproved by him, shall be repassed by two thirds of the Senate and House of Representatives, according to the rules and limitations prescribed in the case of a bill.

Powers Granted to Congress
The Congress shall have the power:

Section 8. To lay and collect taxes, duties, imposts and excises, to pay the debts and provide for the common defense and general welfare of the United States; but all duties, imposts and excises shall be uniform throughout the United States;

To borrow money on the credit of the United States;

To regulate commerce with foreign nations, and among the several states, and with the Indian tribes;

To establish a uniform rule of naturalization, and uniform laws on the subject of bankruptcies throughout the United States;

To coin money, regulate the value thereof, and of foreign coin, and fix the standard of weights and measures;

To provide for the punishment of counterfeiting the securities and current coin of the United States;

To establish post offices and post roads;

To promote the progress of science and useful arts, by securing for limited times to authors and inventors the exclusive right to their respective writings and discoveries;

To constitute tribunals inferior to the Supreme Court;

To define and punish piracies and felonies committed on the high seas, and offenses against the law of nations;

To declare war, grant letters of marque and reprisal, and make rules concerning captures on land and water;

To raise and support armies, but no appropriation of money to that use shall be for a longer term than two years;

To provide and maintain a navy;

To make rules for the government and regulation of the land and naval forces;

To provide for calling forth the militia to execute the laws of the union, suppress insurrections and repel invasions;

To provide for organizing, arming, and disciplining, the militia, and for governing such part of them as may be employed in the service of the United States, reserving to the states respectively, the appointment of the officers, and the authority of training the militia according to the discipline prescribed by Congress;

To exercise exclusive legislation in all cases whatsoever, over such District (not exceeding ten miles square) as may, by cession of particular states, and the acceptance of Congress, become the seat of the government of the United States, and to exercise like authority over all places purchased by the consent of the legislature of the state in which the same shall be, for the erection of forts, magazines, arsenals, dockyards, and other needful buildings;—And

To make all laws which shall be necessary and proper for carrying into execution the foregoing powers, and all other powers vested by this Constitution in the government of the United States, or in any depart-ment or officer thereof.

Powers Forbidden to Congress

Section 9. The migration or importation of such persons as any of the states now existing shall think proper to admit, shall not be prohibited by the Congress prior to the year one thousand eight hundred and eight, but a tax or duty may be imposed on such importation, not exceeding ten dollars for each person.

The privilege of the writ of habeas corpus shall not be suspended, unless when in cases of rebellion or invasion the public safety may require it.

No bill of attainder or ex post facto law shall be passed.

No capitation, [or other direct,] tax shall be laid, unless in proportion to the census or enumeration herein before directed to be taken.

No tax or duty shall be laid on articles exported from any state.

No preference shall be given by any regulation of commerce or revenue to the ports of one state over those of another: nor shall vessels bound to, or from, one state, be obliged to enter, clear or pay duties in another.

No money shall be drawn from the treasury, but in consequence of appropriations made by law; and a regular statement and account of receipts and expenditures of all public money shall be published from time to time.

No title of nobility shall be granted by the United States: and no person holding any office of profit or trust under them, shall, without the consent of the Congress, accept of any present, emolument, office, or title, of any kind whatever, from any king, prince, or foreign state.

Powers Forbidden to the States

Section 10. No state shall enter into any treaty, alliance, or confederation; grant letters of marque and reprisal; coin money; emit bills of credit; make anything but gold and silver coin a tender in payment of debts; pass any bill of attainder, ex post facto law, or law impairing the obligation of contracts, or grant any title of nobility.

No state shall, without the consent of the Congress, lay any imposts or duties on imports or exports, except what may be absolutely necessary for executing its inspection laws: and the net produce of all duties and imposts, laid by any state on imports or exports, shall be for the use of the treasury of the United States; and all such laws shall be subject to the revision and control of the Congress.

No state shall, without the consent of Congress, lay any duty of tonnage, keep troops, or ships of war in time of peace, enter into any agreement or compact with another state, or with a foreign power, or engage in war, unless actually invaded, or in such imminent danger as will not admit of delay.

Article II
The Executive Branch

Section 1. The executive power shall be vested in a President of the United States of America. He shall hold his office during the term of four years, and, together with the Vice President, chosen for the same term, be elected, as follows:

Each state shall appoint, in such manner as the legislature thereof may direct, a number of electors, equal to the whole number of Senators and Representatives to which the State may be entitled in the Congress: but no Senator or Representative, or person holding an office of trust or profit under the United States, shall be appointed an elector.

[The electors shall meet in their respective states, and vote by ballot for two persons, of whom one at least shall not be an inhabitant of the same state with themselves. And they shall make a list of all the persons voted for, and of the number of votes for each; which list they shall sign and certify, and transmit sealed to the seat of the government of the United States, directed to the President of the Senate. The President of the Senate shall, in the presence of the Senate and House of Representatives, open all the certificates, and the votes shall then be counted. The person having the greatest number of votes shall be the President, if such number be a majority of the whole number of electors appointed; and if there be more than one who have such majority, and have an equal number of votes, then the House of Representatives shall immediately choose by ballot one of them for President; and if no person have a majority, then from the five highest on the list the said House shall in like manner choose the President. But in choosing the President, the votes shall be taken by States, the representation from each state having one vote; A quorum for this purpose shall consist of a member or members from two thirds of the states, and a majority of all the states shall be necessary to a choice. In every case, after the choice of the President, the person having the greatest number of votes of the electors shall be the Vice President. But if there should remain two or more who have equal votes, the Senate shall choose from them by ballot the Vice President.]

The Congress may determine the time of choosing the electors, and the day on which they shall give their votes; which day shall be the same throughout the United States.

No person except a natural born citizen, or a citizen of the United States, at the time of the adoption of this Constitution, shall be eligible to the office of President; neither shall any person be eligible to that office who shall not have attained to the age of thirty-five years, and been fourteen Years a resident within the United States.

In case of the removal of the President from office, or of his death, resignation, or inability to discharge the powers and duties of the said office, the same shall devolve on the Vice President, and the Congress may by law provide for the case of removal, death, resignation or inability, both of the President and Vice President, declaring what officer shall then act as President, and such officer shall act accordingly, until the disability be removed, or a President shall be elected.

The President shall, at stated times, receive for his services, a compensation, which shall neither be increased nor diminished during the period for which he shall have been elected, and he shall not receive within that period any other emolument from the United States, or any of them.

Before he enter on the execution of his office, he shall take the following oath or affirmation:—"I do solemnly swear (or affirm) that I will faithfully execute the office of President of the United States, and will to the best of my ability, preserve, protect and defend the Constitution of the United States."

Section 2. The President shall be commander-in-chief of the Army and Navy of the United States, and of the militia of the several states, when called into the actual service of the United States; he may require the opinion, in writing, of the principal officer in each of the executive departments, upon any subject relating to the duties of their respective offices, and he shall have power to grant reprieves and pardons for offenses against the United States, except in cases of impeachment.

He shall have power, by and with the advice and consent of the Senate, to make treaties, provided two-thirds of the Senators present concur; and he shall nominate, and by and with the advice and consent of the Senate, shall appoint ambassadors, other public ministers and consuls, judges of the Supreme Court, and all other officers of the United States, whose appointments are not herein otherwise provided for, and which shall be established by law: but the Congress may by law vest the appointment of such inferior officers, as they think proper, in the President alone, in the courts of law, or in the heads of departments.

The President shall have power to fill up all vacancies that may happen during the recess of the Senate, by granting commissions which shall expire at the end of their next session.

Section 3. He shall from time to time give to the Congress information of the state of the union, and recommend to their consideration such measures as he shall judge necessary and expedient; he may, on extraordinary occasions, convene both Houses, or either of them, and in case of disagreement between them, with respect to the time of adjournment, he may adjourn them to such time as he shall think proper; he shall receive ambassadors and other public ministers; he shall take care that the laws be faithfully executed, and shall commission all the officers of the United States.

Section 4. The President, Vice President and all civil officers of the United States, shall be removed from office on impeachment for, and conviction of, treason, bribery, or other high crimes and misdemeanors.

Article III
The Judicial Branch

Section 1. The judicial power of the United States, shall be vested in one Supreme Court, and in such inferior courts as the Congress may from time to time ordain and establish. The judges, both of the supreme and inferior courts, shall hold their offices during good behaviour, and shall, at stated times, receive for their services, a compensation, which shall not be diminished during their continuance in office.

Section 2. The judicial power shall extend to all cases, in law and equity, arising under this Constitution, the laws of the United States, and treaties made, or which shall be made, under their authority;—to all cases affecting ambassadors, other public ministers and consuls;—to all cases of admiralty and maritime jurisdiction, [—to controversies to which the United States shall be a party;—to controversies between two or more states, [between a state and citizens of another state;], between citizens of different states;—between citizens of the same state, claiming lands under grants of different states, and between a state, or the citizens thereof, and foreign states, [citizens or subjects].

In all cases affecting ambassadors, other public ministers and consuls, and those in which a state shall be party, the Supreme Court shall have original jurisdiction. In all the other cases before mentioned, the Supreme Court shall have appellate jurisdiction, both as to law and fact, with such exceptions, and under such regulations as the Congress shall make.

The trial of all crimes, except in cases of impeach-ment, shall be by jury; and such trial shall be held in the state where the said crimes shall have been committed; but when not committed within any state, the trial shall be at such place or places as the Congress may by law have directed.

Section 3. Treason against the United States, shall consist only in levying war against them, or in adhering to their enemies, giving them aid and comfort. No person shall be convicted of treason unless on the testimony of two witnesses to the same overt act, or on confession in open court.

The Congress shall have power to declare the punishment of treason, but no attainder of treason shall work corruption of blood, or forfeiture except during the life of the person attainted.

Article IV
Relation of the States to Each Other

Section 1. Full faith and credit shall be given in each state to the public acts, records, and judicial proceedings of every other state. And the Congress may by general laws prescribe the manner in which such acts, records, and proceedings shall be proved, and the effect thereof.

Section 2. The citizens of each state shall be entitled to all privileges and immunities of citizens in the several states.

person charged in any state with treason, felony, or other crime, who shall flee from justice, and be found in another state, shall on demand of the executive authority of the state from which he fled, be delivered up, to be removed to the state having jurisdiction of the crime.

[No person held to service or labor in one state, under the laws thereof, escaping into another, shall, in consequence of any law or regulation therein, be discharged from such service or labor, but shall be delivered up on claim of the party to whom such service or labor may be due.]

Federal-State Relations

Section 3. New states may be admitted by the Congress into this Union; but no new states shall be formed or erected within the jurisdiction of any other state, nor any state be formed by the junction of two or more states, without the consent of the legislatures of the states concerned, as well as of the Congress.

The Congress shall have power to dispose of and make all needful rules and regulations respecting the territory or other property belonging to the United States; and nothing in this Constitution shall be so construed as to prejudice any claims of the United States, or of any particular state.

Section 4. The United States shall guarantee to every state in this union a republican form of government, and shall protect each of them against invasion; and on application of the legislature, or of the executive (when the legislature cannot be convened) against domestic violence.

Article V
Amending the Constitution

The Congress, whenever two thirds of both houses shall deem it necessary, shall propose amendments to this Constitution, or, on the application of the legislatures of two thirds of the several states, shall call a convention for proposing amendments, which, in either case, shall be valid to all intents and purposes, as part of this Constitution, when ratified by the legislatures of three fourths of the several states, or by conventions in three fourths thereof, as the one or the other mode of ratification may be proposed by the Congress; provided [that no amendment which may be made prior to the year one thousand eight hundred and eight shall in any manner affect the first and fourth clauses in the ninth section of the first article; and] that no state, without its consent, shall be deprived of its equal suffrage in the Senate.

Article VI
National Debts

All debts contracted and engagements entered into, before the adoption of this Constitution, shall be as valid against the United States under this Constitution, as under the Confederation.

Supremacy of the National Government

This Constitution, and the laws of the United States which shall be made in pursuance thereof; and all treaties made, or which shall be made, under the authority of the United States, shall be the supreme law of the land; and the judges in every state shall be bound thereby, anything in the constitution or laws of any State to the contrary notwithstanding.

The senators and representatives before mentioned, and the members of the several state legislatures, and all executive and judicial officers, both of the United States and of the several states, shall be bound by oath or affirmation, to support this Constitution; but no religious test shall ever be required as a qualification to any office or public trust under the United States.

Article VII
Ratifying the Constitution

The ratification of the conventions of nine states, shall be sufficient for the establishment of this Constitution between the states so ratifying the same.

Done in convention by the unanimous consent of the states present the seventeenth day of September in the year of our Lord one thousand seven hundred and eighty seven and of the independence of the United States of America the twelfth. In witness whereof we have hereunto subscribed our Names.

Amendment XVIII

Section 1. After one year from the ratification of this article the manufacture, sale, or transportation of intoxicating liquors within, the importation thereof into, or the exportation thereof from the United States and all the territory subject to the jurisdiction thereof for beverage purposes is hereby prohibited.

Section 2. The Congress and the several States shall have concurrent power to enforce this article by appropriate legislation.

Section 3. This article shall be inoperative unless it shall have been ratified as an amendment to the Constitution by the legislatures of the several States, as provided in the Constitution, within seven years from the date of the submission hereof to the States by the Congress.

Amendment XXI

Section 1. The eighteenth article of amendment to the Constitution of the United States is hereby repealed.

Section 2. The transportation or importation into any State, Territory, or possession of the United States for delivery or use therein of intoxicating liquors, in violation of the laws thereof, is hereby prohibited.

Section 3. This article shall be inoperative unless it shall have been ratified as an amendment to the Constitution by conventions in the several States, as provided in the Constitution, within seven years from the date of the submission hereof to the States by the Congress.

The Internet sites described below can be accessed at http://www.myreportlinks.com

▶**The Charters of Freedom: The Constitution**
Editor's Choice Read the U.S. Constitution on the National Archives Web site.

▶**Alcohol, Temperance and Prohibition**
Editor's Choice Explore the Prohibition era through this Brown University Library Web site.

▶**The Dry Years**
Editor's Choice Images relating to Prohibition are available on this Web site.

▶**Teaching With Documents: The Volstead Act and Related Prohibition Documents**
Editor's Choice Documents related to Prohibition can be found on the National Archives site.

▶**Today in History: October 28**
Editor's Choice The Library of Congress presents this page on the history of the antialcohol lobby.

▶*Temperance & Prohibition*
Editor's Choice Ohio State University's eHistory series takes a look at the antialcohol movement.

▶**Al Capone Museum**
Take a multimedia journey to learn more about Al Capone.

▶**Alcohol Prohibition Was a Failure**
Read an essay that explores the legacy of Prohibition on this site.

▶**Alphonse Capone, aka. Al, Scarface**
The FBI Web site provides this short history of Al Capone.

▶**The American Mafia: History of the Mafia**
View a time line highlighting Prohibition and the mob on this site.

▶**Anti-Saloon League 1893–1933**
Learn about the Anti-Saloon League from this Web site.

▶**Anti-Saloon League of America**
Read this short overview of the Anti-Saloon League of America.

▶**Branches of Government**
Learn how the federal government works at this Web site.

▶**Chicago in the Roaring Twenties**
Find an overview of Chicago in the 1920s on this Web site.

▶**Crime Library: Prohibition and a Murky Beginning**
This series of articles looks at Rhode Island in the Prohibition days.

Report Links

The Internet sites described below can be accessed at http://www.myreportlinks.com

▶**Early Industrialization**
The Industrial Revolution is chronicled on this site.

▶**Exploring Constitutional Law**
The University of Missouri-Kansas City Law School presents this Web site.

▶**Franklin D. Roosevelt Presidential Library and Museum**
Learn more about the thirty-second president of the United States.

▶**Herbert Hoover Presidential Library & Museum: The Great Depression**
Learn about the Great Depression at this Web site.

▶**History of Anti-Alcohol Movements in the U.S.**
The State University of New York provides a good overview of temperance activists.

▶**Progressive Protestantism: The Life of Frances Willard, 1839–1896**
This is a biography of Frances Willard.

▶**Records of the Wickersham Commission on Law Observance and Enforcement**
A description of the Wickersham Commission records can be found on this site.

▶**Schaffer Library of Drug Policy: Adopting National Prohibition**
A lengthy history of the crusade to abolish the use of alcohol can be found on this site.

▶**U.S. Constitution: Eighteenth Amendment**
Text of the Eighteenth Amendment is available on this Web site.

▶**U.S. Constitution: Twenty-First Amendment**
Text of the Twenty-First Amendment is posted on this site.

▶*The Use and Need of the Life of Carry A. Nation*
Read the autobiography of Carry A. Nation on this Web site.

▶**We Want Beer: Prohibition and the Will to Imbibe**
This is an essay on how brewery owners won one war but lost another.

▶**Whiskey Rebellion: Whiskey Insurrection**
The Whiskey Rebellion and its leaders are covered on this Web site.

▶**Woman's Christian Temperance Union**
Learn about how this historical organization promoted and fought for temperance.

▶**Woodrow Wilson**
This PBS Web site puts the spotlight on President Woodrow Wilson.

alcoholic—An addicted person who continually and uncontrollably drinks more alcohol than what is considered normal use. Alcoholism is often considered a disease.

amendment—A change that fixes or adds something.

appeal—A case for which a higher court has determined it should review the decision, or a process in which a lawyer asks a higher court to review an unfavorable decision.

black market—The trade of illegal or contraband goods.

bootlegger—A person who sells liquor when it is against the law.

brewer—A person who makes beer.

census—A count of the people who live in a country.

conserve—Use as little as possible. Use without wasting any.

constitution—The basic laws upon which a nation is founded.

contraband—Goods that are brought into a country illegally.

distill—Make whiskey and other liquors.

dry—A person who supported prohibition.

flapper—A stylish young woman in the 1920s.

imbibe—To drink or to have soak in. Usually used to describe the drinking of alcohol.

industrial—Having to do with factories and the things they make.

intoxicate—Make drunk from alcohol.

legislature—A body of lawmakers.

lobby—Try to get members of Congress to vote in a particular way on an issue.

moonshine—Illegally made liquor.

prescription—A doctor's written orders for a remedy or drug.

profit—The money that is left over after all the costs of running a business are paid.

prohibition—A law that banned the making and selling of alcoholic beverages

ratify—Agree to make into a law.

referendum—A vote in which the citizens get to decide on a law or other measure.

reform—Try to improve something by changing it.

repeal—To take away or revoke. To overturn a law that has been deemed ineffective.

saloon—A place where liquor is sold and drunk.

smuggle—Secretly bring illegal goods into a country.

speakeasy—A place where illegal liquor was sold and drunk during Prohibition.

still—A device that is used to distill liquor.

tax—Money that people pay to the government.

teetotaler—A person who has made a pledge not to drink any alcohol.

temperance—The avoidance of drinking alcohol, especially to excess.

wet—A person who did not agree with Prohibition.

whiskey—A strong alcoholic drink made from grains like corn and rye.

Chapter 1. Women Unite Against the Demon Rum

1. David E. Kyvig, ed., *Law, Alcohol, and Order: Perspectives on National Prohibition* (Westport, Conn.: Greenwood Press, 1985), p. 7.

2. John Kobler, *Ardent Spirits: The Rise and Fall of Prohibition* (New York: Da Capo Press, 1993), p. 117.

3. Kathleen Drowne, *Spirits of Defiance: National Prohibition and Jazz Age Literature, 1920–1933* (Columbus: Ohio State University Press, 2005), pp. 14–15.

4. Frances Willard, as quoted in Ruth Bordin, *Frances Willard: A Biography* (Chapel Hill: The University of North Carolina Press, 1986), p. 98.

5. Kobler, p. 204.

Chapter 2. Temperance and Teetotalers

1. Sean Dennis Cashman, *Prohibition: The Lie of the Land* (New York: The Free Press, 1981), p. 3.

2. J.C. Furnas, *The Life and Times of the Late Demon Rum* (New York: G.P. Putnam's and Sons, 1965), pp. 162–163.

3. Cashman, pp. 5–6.

4. Furnas, p. 157.

5. John Kobler, *Ardent Spirits: The Rise and Fall of Prohibition* (New York: G.P. Putnam's Sons, 1973), p. 181.

6. Charles Merz, *The Dry Decade* (Seattle: University of Washington Press, 1969), p. 27.

Chapter 3. The Death of John Barleycorn

1. John Kobler, *Ardent Spirits: The Rise and Fall of Prohibition* (New York: G.P. Putnam's Sons, 1973), p. 200.

2. Charles Merz, *The Dry Decade* (Seattle: University of Washington Press, 1969), p. 16.

3. David E. Kyvig, *Repealing National Prohibition* (Kent, Ohio: Kent State University Press, 2000), p. 13.

4. Merz, p. 1.

5. Ibid., p. 333.

6. Thomas R. Pegram, *Battling Demon Rum: The Struggle for a Dry America, 1800–1933* (Chicago: Ivan R. Dee, 1998), p. 161.

7. Kathleen Drowne, *Spirits of Defiance: National Prohibition and Jazz Age Literature, 1920–1933* (Columbus: Ohio State University Press, 2005), p. 50.

8. Kyvig, p.29.

9. Sean Dennis Cashman, *Prohibition: The Lie of the Land* (New York: The Free Press, 1981), pp. 50–51.

Chapter 4. Speakeasies, Moonshining, and Bootleggers

1. Sean Dennis Cashman, *Prohibition: The Lie of the Land* (New York: The Free Press, 1981), p. 81.

2. Al Capone, as quoted in David E. Kyvig, *Repealing National Prohibition* (Kent, Ohio: Kent State University Press, 2000), p. 26.

3. John Kobler, *Ardent Spirits: the Rise and Fall of Prohibition* (New York: G.P. Putnam's Sons, 1973), p. 257.

4. Ibid., p. 241.

5. Kathleen Drowne, *Spirits of Defiance: National Prohibition and Jazz Age Literature, 1920–1933* (Columbus: Ohio State University Press, 2005), p. 29.

6. Charles Merz, *The Dry Decade* (Seattle: University of Washington Press, 1969), pp. 85–86.

7. Drowne, p. 155.

8. Thomas R. Pegram, *Battling Demon Rum: The Struggle for a Dry America, 1890–1933* (Chicago: Ivan R. Dee, 1998), p. 176.

Chapter 5. Prohibition in the Courts

1. Thomas R. Pegram, *Battling Demon Rum: The Struggle for a Dry America, 1890–1933* (Chicago: Ivan R. Dee, 1998), p. 157.

2. Charles Merz, *The Dry Decade* (Seattle: University of Washington Press, 1969), pp. 276–277.

3. David E. Kyvig, *Repealing National Prohibition* (Kent, Ohio: Kent State University Press, 2000), p. 32.

4. Ibid., p. 18.

5. David E. Kyvig, "Sober Thoughts: Myths and Realities of National Prohibition after Fifty Years," *Law, Alcohol, and Order: Perspectives on National Prohibition* (Westport, Conn.: Greenwood Press, 1985), p. 11.

6. Kyvig, *Repealing National Prohibition,* p. 35.

7. Paul L. Murphy, "Societal Morality and Individual Freedom," *Law, Alcohol, and Order: Perspectives on National Prohibition* (Westport, Conn.: Greenwood Press, 1985), p. 77.

8. Committee on the Judiciary, Subcommittee

on the Constitution, United States Senate. *Amendments to the Constitution: A Brief Legislative History* (Washington: U.S. Government Printing Office, 1985), p. 66.

Chapter 6. The End of a Noble Experiment

1. David E. Kyvig, *Repealing National Prohibition* (Kent, Ohio: Kent State University Press, 2000), p. 39.

2. Pauline Sabin as quoted in Sean Dennis Cashman, *Prohibition: The Lie of the Land* (New York: The Free Press, 1981), pp. 159–160.

3. Morris Sheppard, as quoted in Charles Merz, *The Dry Decade* (Seattle: University of Washington Press, 1969), p. 297.

4. President Herbert Hoover, as quoted in David E. Kyvig, ed. *Law, Alcohol, and Order* (Westport, Conn.: Greenwood Press, 1985), p. 4.

5. Kyvig, p. 201.

6. Sean Dennis Cashman, *Prohibition: The Lie of the Land* (New York: The Free Press, 1981), pp. 238–239.

7. The National Organization for the Reform of Marijuana Laws, "Frequently Asked Questions," *NORML: Working to Reform Marijuana Laws,* n.d., <http://www.norml.org/index.cfm?Group_ID= 3418> (June 11, 2006).

8. NCERx Medical Editorial Board, "Red Wine in Moderation Can Have a Positive Effect on Health," *Red Wine and Health,* October 24, 2006, <http://www.red-wine-and-health.com/> (June 11, 2006).

9. Bureau of Justice Statistics, "General Statistics," *Mothers Against Drunk Driving,* n.d., <http://www.madd.org/stats/1789> (June 11, 2006).

10. National Highway Traffic Safety Administration, "State-By-State Traffic Fatalities-2004," *Mothers Against Drunk Driving,* n.d., <http://www.madd.org/stats/10213> (June 11, 2006)

Bingham, Jane. *Alcohol (What's the Deal?)*. Chicago, Ill.: Heinemann Library, 2005.

Doak, Robin. *Franklin D. Roosevelt*. Milwaukee, Wis.: World Almanac Library, 2002.

Erickson, John R. *Moonshiner's Gold*. New York: Viking, 2001.

Freedman, Russell. *Children of the Great Depression*. New York: Clarion Books, 2005.

Harvey, Bonnie C. *Carry A. Nation: Saloon Smasher and Prohibitionist*. Berkeley Heights, N.J.: Enslow Publishers, Inc., 2002.

Hill, Jeff. *Prohibition*. Detroit: Omnigraphics, 2004.

Lieurance, Suzanne. *The Prohibition Era in American History*. Berkeley Heights, N.J.: Enslow Publishers, Inc., 2003.

Ruggiero, Adriane. *World War I*. Tarrytown, N.Y.: Benchmark Books, 2003.

Swisher, Clarice. *Women of the Roaring Twenties*. San Diego: Lucent Books, 2005.

Weatherly, Myra, ed. *Living in 1920s America*. San Diego: Greenhaven Press, 2005.

Yancy, Diane. *Al Capone*. San Diego: Lucent Books, 2003.

DATE DUE

'09			
APR 12			
DEC 16			
JAN 04			
MAR 21			